COACHING

WALKTHRUs

BETTER COACHING STEP BY STEP

&

MATT STONE
TOM SHERRINGTON
OLIVER CAVIGLIOLI

To order, please visit www.HachetteLearning.com or contact Customer Service at education@hachette.co.uk / +44 (0)1235 827827.

ISBN: 9781036007270

First published in 2025 by
Hachette Learning,
An Hachette UK Company
Carmelite House
50 Victoria Embankment
London EC4Y 0DZ

www.HachetteLearning.com

The authorised representative in the EEA is Hachette Ireland, 8 Castlecourt Centre, Dublin 15, D15 XTP3, Ireland (email: info@hbgi.ie)

Impression 10 9 8 7 6 5 4 3 2 1

Year 2029 2028 2027 2026 2025

A catalogue record for this title is available from the British Library

Printed in the UK

YAVOR DJONEV

Founder of Foundation for Educational Transformation and the Bulgarian Progressive Schools, Bulgaria

The *Teaching WalkThrus* have been the backbone of our Teacher Competency Model and PD Programme for several years now. They provide a clear and precise professional language that drives improvement forward. The *Coaching WalkThrus* will certainly be an effectiveness multiplier.

JUDE ARKWRIGHT

Headteacher, St Michael's CE VA Primary School, England

Coaching WalkThrus provides dedicated time to think about being a better teacher, with opportunities to practise techniques in front of colleagues. It celebrates the process of improvement and supports a whole-school approach to CPD that is rich in content. The programme delivers immediate and sustainable impact, with something valuable for every teacher and leader.

BRUCE ROBERTSON

Director of Next Level Foundation, author of *The Teaching Delusion* trilogy, Scotland

Coaching WalkThrus is an excellent resource for any school or team interested in coaching approaches to professional development. It is very clear and offers a wide range of practical strategies that all schools should find valuable to consider. Whether you are new to coaching or looking to refine your existing approaches, you are likely to find *Coaching WalkThrus* extremely useful.

BRON RYRIE JONES

Teacher Educator & Instructional Coach, Australia

Coaching WalkThrus is a must-read for coaches who want to work with rigour, warmth and the spirit of collegiality. As we've come to expect from the WalkThrus team, this is yet another handbag-sized gift to the field.

FLO WEIR

Deputy Headteacher Verwood CE First School and Nursery

The WalkThrus have supported us to build a shared and consistent language around pedagogy and coaching. The depth of the techniques has fuelled teacher confidence to have meaningful discussions about their practice and ensure that precision and purpose are at the heart of our professional development.

VALENTINA DEVID

Author & Trainer, Toetsrevolutie, the Netherlands

What a breath of fresh air this book is. Practical, hands-on and straight to the point – exactly what you need when working in coaching. It offers a comprehensive overview of what really matters and brings clarity to your own approach. I found it genuinely enriching: things I was already doing intuitively now have names, structure and categories. That alone makes my practice more focused and effective.

MATT STONE

Matt spent 15 years as an English teacher and senior leader in south Wales, during which time he also worked across the region to support schools in designing and implementing coaching programmes. Matt now works with the WalkThrus team, supporting schools and systems in the UK and beyond to implement evidence-informed approaches to teaching and professional development. *Coaching WalkThrus* is his first book, co-authored with Tom and Oliver.

TOM SHERRINGTON

Tom was a teacher and school leader for 30 years and now, as co-director of Teaching WalkThrus, works with schools around the world to design and implement effective professional development programmes. Drawing on his classroom and consultancy experience, he has written several books for teachers including the WalkThrus series with Oliver and *Rosenshine's Principles in Action.* Tom enjoys presenting at educational conferences including the magnificent researchED events.

OLIVER CAVIGLIOLI

Oliver was a special school headteacher before stepping into training, writing and illustrating. His special school background was the platform for his pursuit of depicting ideas visually. Twenty-five years ago, he wrote a series of books on visual learning strategies. More recently, he wrote *Dual Coding with Teachers* and *Organise Ideas* with David Goodwin. He has designed and illustrated the books of leading educational authors that include Tom Sherrington, Paul Kirschner and the Learning Scientists.

We would like to extend a special thanks to our guest contributors: Nikki Sullivan, Sarah Cottinghatt, Adam Kohlbeck and Josh Goodrich. We're so grateful to have you share your expertise. In fact, we owe a debt of gratitude to the many researchers, leaders and coaches who have generously shared their wisdom; to the schools and colleges who have welcomed us in and embraced our approaches; to each other, of course; and to our families, for their unwavering support and encouragement.

INTRODUCTION

This book began as a companion to our *Teaching WalkThrus* series — a resource for the thousands of schools in our growing community. But it's become something more. *Coaching WalkThrus* is for anyone with the responsibility of helping teachers get better — coaches, mentors, team leaders, senior leaders. Helping teachers navigate the complexity of the classroom takes a balance of support and accountability — it can be a challenge to get this right. Teachers improve when leaders and coaches work shoulder to shoulder with them to seek out learning problems, work on tried and tested solutions, model and rehearse techniques until they're ready for the classroom, and help make changes stick. The same applies to teaching assistants — this book is for them too.

Coaching WalkThrus is presented in four sections:

WHY? brings together key ideas that underpin the coaching guides in this book — some drawn from our own fieldwork and others from influential research into teacher expertise.

HOW? outlines the design decisions, structures and processes that make coaching realistic and sustainable. It shares lessons from our work with schools and colleges, alongside clear implementation guidance for leaders, coaches and teachers.

WHAT? includes nearly 50 techniques for coaches, organised across the six phases of the **WalkThrus Coaching Process** (see opposite). These ultra-practical guides are for new and experienced coaches, and for leaders implementing coaching in schools or teams. We're strong advocates of Paul Bambrick-Santoyo's 5Ps feedback framework — you'll find this referenced throughout the book. We explore this more fully in the Feedback & Support chapter.

SCENARIOS offers practical guidance for navigating common situations you might encounter as a coach. Each WalkThru helps you to adapt the ideas in this book to your context, while staying focused on purposeful, respectful improvement.

This book is a collection of 70+ step-by-step visual guides, grounded in our extensive fieldwork with schools, designed to help coaches do the job well, with both humility and purpose.

WALKTHRUs COACHING PROCESS

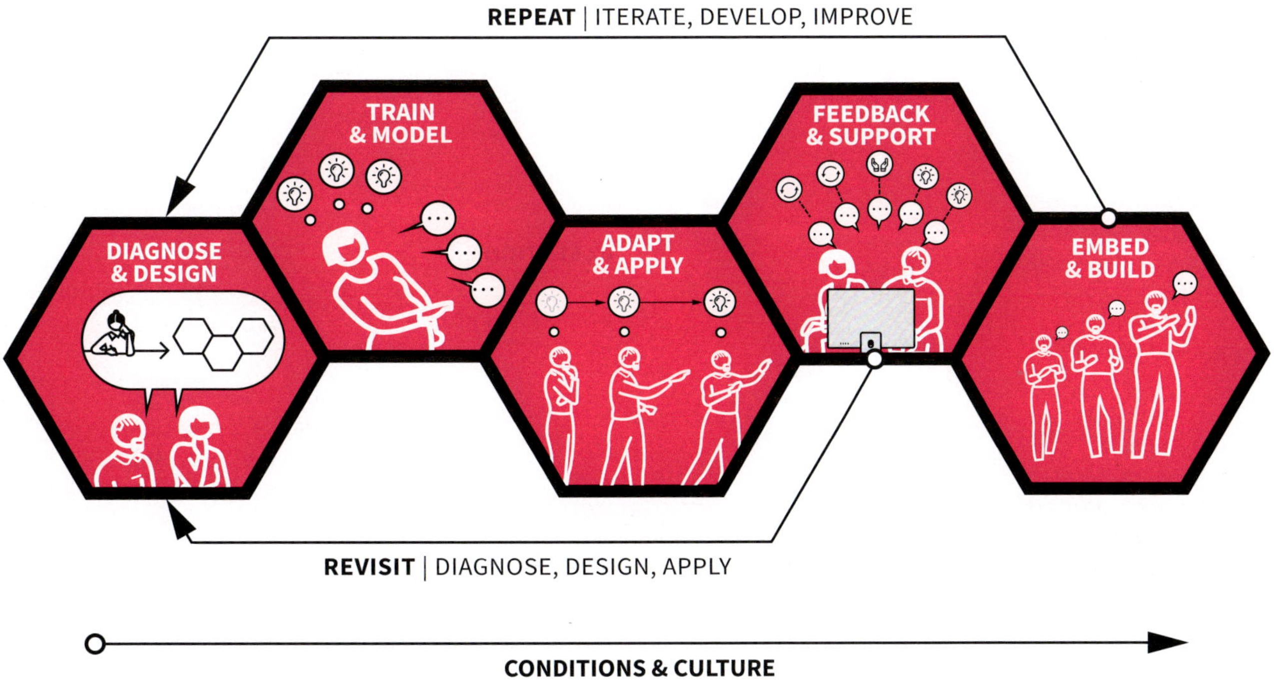

CONTENTS

WALKTHRU SECTIONS

WHY?

Coaching works best when grounded in a clear understanding of how teachers learn, what effective teaching involves and why some approaches to PD are more likely to make a difference. The Why? section brings together key ideas that underpin the coaching practices in this book. Some come from our own fieldwork, others from influential researchers in the field of teacher expertise. It also serves as a useful companion to the Why? sections of our *Teaching WalkThrus* series.

MEANINGFUL COACHING

Coaching only matters if it changes what happens when no one is watching. Teachers spend 98% of their time alone in the classroom, making real-time decisions. If coaching doesn't shape that time, it's wasted. Meaningful coaching works on three levels:

PERSONAL | It solves problems teachers care about.

COGNITIVE | It helps them think clearly about their practice.

TECHNICAL | It sharpens their use of core teaching techniques.

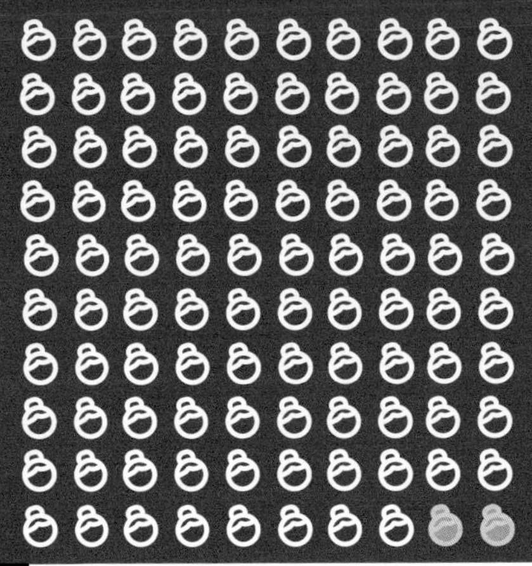

1

THE 98% PROBLEM

Teachers spend 95-98% of their time alone with students, making their own decisions, in the moment. Coaching is only meaningful if it changes what happens when no one is watching. Focus on the 98%.

Coaching should give teachers mental models that help them to intentionally create the conditions for learning, not just ideas that work in theory. If it doesn't stick when the door closes, it doesn't matter.

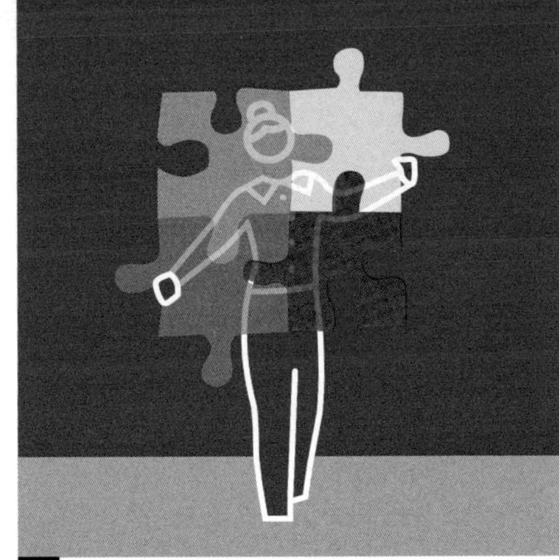

2

PERSONAL

Teachers commit to change when it feels relevant and worthwhile. Coaching should solve problems they recognise in their classrooms — things that make learning better for them and their students.

Make it personal, even in group coaching. Show respect for their expertise by working with them, not imposing solutions. When teachers see the value, they'll invest.

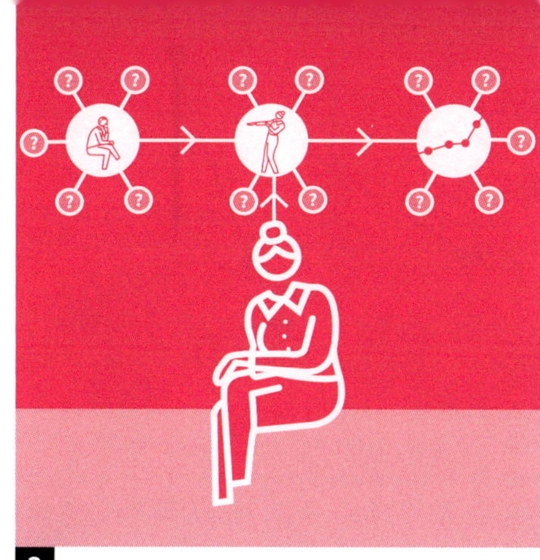

3

COGNITIVE

Teachers need time to think clearly about their practice. They need space to process what they see, question their decisions and sharpen their judgement.

A coach's job is to help organise thinking, build awareness and make sense of the classroom. Ask the right questions. Surface useful insights. Make it easier for teachers to see, understand and act.

4

TECHNICAL

Teaching is a craft. Mastering core techniques gives teachers more control, more options and better responses to classroom challenges.

Coaching should focus on what works and when to use it. Help teachers build a toolkit of techniques — then sharpen their intentionality about applying them at the right moments.

5

THE SWEET SPOT

Meaningful coaching balances personal, cognitive and technical support. The sweet spot is where these overlap. Teachers feel respected and motivated. They have time to think. They gain practical tools they know how to use.

Get this right, and coaching makes a real difference.

PD MECHANISMS | WHY COACHING WORKS

As discussed in *WalkThrus Volume 3*, the EEF report *Effective Professional Development* (2021) concluded that PD can be effective in many forms provided that certain key processes they call *mechanisms* are involved. They identify 14 such mechanisms in four areas, each of which serves a specific function.

If we view coaching as one element in a wider programme, it's helpful to explore the extent to which the process delivers each of these mechanisms, underlining the rationale for investing our time in a good coaching system.

1

BUILD KNOWLEDGE

- **MANAGING COGNITIVE LOAD**
- **REVISITING PRIOR LEARNING**

The coaching process allows a teacher at any career stage to continually build up their knowledge, step by step, always revisiting and consolidating prior learning over time. Shrewd analysis of teaching problems can allow a very sharp focus area to be identified, with specific steps to work on. Knowledge of curriculum and assessment accumulates over years so coaches should guide this as a very long-run goal.

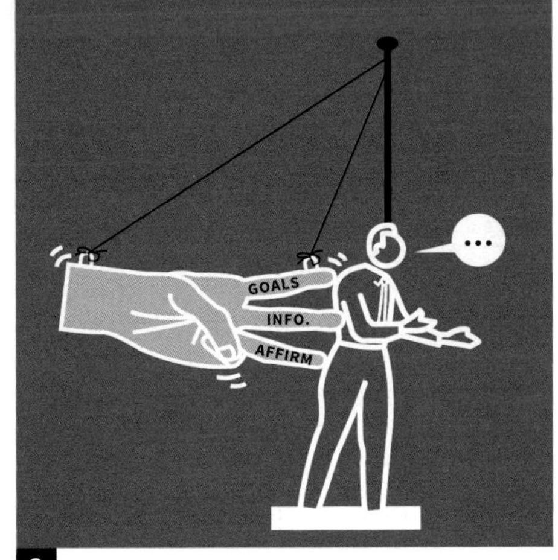

2

MOTIVATE STAFF

- **SETTING AND AGREEING ON GOALS**
- **PRESENTING INFORMATION FROM A CREDIBLE SOURCE**
- **PROVIDING AFFIRMATION & REINFORCEMENT AFTER PROGRESS**

Coaching should support all three forms:

- Setting appropriately challenging goals each session with the expectation of serious engagement in attempting to meet them.
- Offering credible suggestions and asking intelligent questions.
- Making teachers feel good about their work and the progress they're making.

3

DEVELOP TEACHING TECHNIQUES

- INSTRUCTION
- SOCIAL SUPPORT
- MODELLING
- MONITORING & FEEDBACK
- REHEARSAL

Coaching should be highly technical in terms of establishing a shared understanding of the learning problems and the precision of each technique under discussion. This can be achieved with an element of modelling by the coach or by reference to videos or the WalkThrus resources. Rehearsal also forms part of the overall sequence, with feedback forming a key element of any coaching cycle.

4

EMBED PRACTICE

- PROVIDING PROMPTS AND CUES
- PROMPTING ACTION PLANNING
- ENCOURAGING MONITORING
- PROMPTING CONTEXT-SPECIFIC REPETITION

To support embedding of practice, coaching has to be sustained. Over several iterative cycles of observation and feedback, the coach can focus on how well the teacher sustains techniques over time, building new habits, beyond merely enacting techniques in a performative style every so often. WalkThrus steps provide both coach and teacher with a set of prompts to support deeper habits to form and become embedded.

5

TAKE ACCOUNT OF CONTEXT, NEEDS & TIME CONSTRAINTS

The 14 mechanisms only really work if they can be applied in the specific context a teacher and coach are working in. The design of a coaching cycle including the frequency of observation and time given for feedback conversations has to be woven into the fabric of the school calendar, adapted to fit whatever time is available.

Coaching concepts built on assumptions of elements of school culture need to be modified to fit the prevailing realities, maximising the impact in the conditions as they are.

THE LEARNING MODEL | STUDENTS

Since the ultimate goal in supporting a teacher is to improve the learning of the teacher's students, it's vital to have a shared understanding of how learning happens.

Lesson observations, co-constructed feedback and action planning should all reference the rationale for any given strategy or technique, rooted in an evidence base from research and good knowledge of the learning process.

All our WalkThrus techniques are informed by a simple learning model derived from the work of Dan Willingham and cognitive load theory more generally.

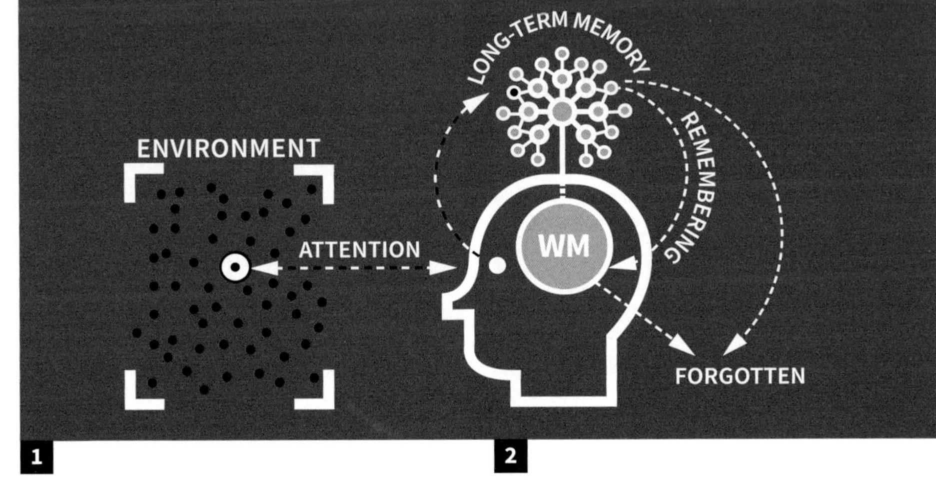

1

COGNITIVE ARCHITECTURE

WORKING MEMORY | Our finite capacity has implications for breaking ideas down into small chunks and for how we present information:

- Transient information — e.g. extensive talk or slides no longer visible can be hard to process.
- Excessive information can quickly overload students.

LONG-TERM MEMORY | Each student has their own schema; relevant knowledge needs to be activated to enter working memory so that it can be built on.

2

ATTENTION

Students need to learn consciously, using their working memory to select and organise information, then integrate it with their existing schema for the material in hand. This requires deliberate effort with students directing their attention to the learning process underway.

However, in the absence of routines or activities that require students to focus their attention, they easily drift. It's natural and inevitable. How to engage all students' attention is a key focus for many teachers.

3

THINKING

A key concept from Willingham is *memory is the residue of thought*. A good rule of thumb is that without thinking, there is no learning, so every individual student must engage in their own thinking. This has implications for task design:

- Does every student have a chance to think?
- Are they all expected to think? How does the teacher check?
- Do the tasks require thinking about the concepts?
- Do students have the prior knowledge needed to do the thinking?

4

MAKING MEANING

A vital idea in learning is that, even when presented with the same material in the same way, students will always make sense of the concepts in their own way because each person's specific schema or prior knowledge is unique to them. This is entirely normal and usually unproblematic but sometimes a student's meaning includes serious misconceptions or significant gaps.

A key task of teaching is to explore the meaning students have actually made — through tasks and dialogue where their understanding is revealed — then seeking to address issues that emerge.

5

CONSOLIDATION & PRACTICE

Learning that develops with new concepts or skills can be very tenuous. It is very easy to forget material soon after completing a task unless students engage in some form of practice that allows them to consolidate their learning, strengthening connections between their prior knowledge and anything new.

Another key aspect of teaching to discuss is how well all students in a class are able to engage in practice tasks — repeating or revisiting material multiple times, undertaking retrieval practice and building fluency.

THE LEARNING MODEL | TEACHERS

All teachers engaged in professional development are also learners in that context so it's logical that ideas from our learning model will apply to the process, with implications for coaching.

If, as coaches, we understand the reasons why teachers might struggle with a concept or not change their habits over time, we are better placed to anticipate the issues and to address them.

A coach benefits from having a good mental model for teacher learning to support their decision-making over the course of a coaching sequence.

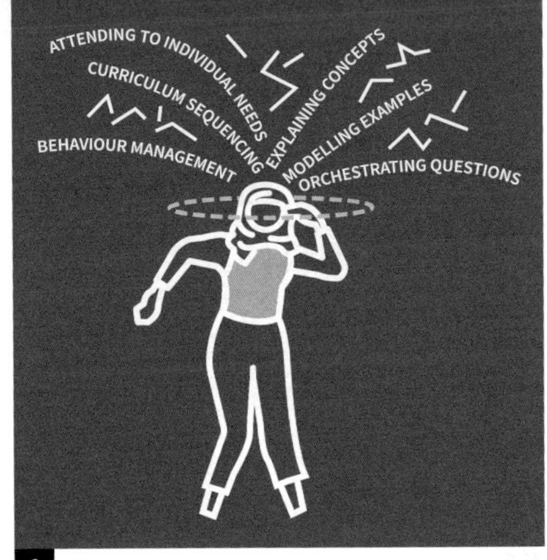

1

COGNITIVE LOAD

Teachers all experience the challenge of overloading their working memory. There are only so many things we can think about at once and teachers often have a lot on their plate: behaviour management, curriculum sequencing, explaining concepts and modelling examples, orchestrating questioning, attending to the needs of individual students — it's complex.

Coaching is best when teachers focus on specific elements in the complexity, reducing the scope of the challenge and breaking techniques down into small steps.

2

SCHEMA BUILDING

Knowledge of each aspect of teaching — behaviour, curriculum, explaining, questioning, assessment — will build gradually over time. Teachers will have a range of prior knowledge and experience that forms the platform for any new learning.

Each teacher's schema will be unique to them so coaches need to avoid assuming the presence or absence of certain knowledge; they should ask appropriate questions to explore the teacher's understanding as part of their dialogue, supporting them to make connections to what they've learned before.

3

MEANING MAKING

Even where routines seem reasonably tightly defined, each teacher engaging with them will make sense of the steps in their own way — locating them within their context, applied to their students, subject and teaching space. There's a risk a coach might assume that a teacher has the same mental model as they do when actually their view is different in an important way.

Questions that form part of a coaching conversation should seek to explore how a teacher has made sense of ideas themselves; it's the teacher's model that matters, not the coach's.

4

PRACTICE & CONSOLIDATION

As with learning any new knowledge or skill, there's always a risk that teaching techniques can deviate from the original idea or be forgotten completely in the absence of repeated practice.

In any coaching sequence an emphasis on practice is helpful, with feedback focused on the degree of precision or fluency. This can influence decisions about when to move on from one focus area to another. Often it's a better bet to stay focused on one aspect for longer, to allow more time for consolidation, rather than trying to move on too soon to something else.

5

FLUENCY

Teachers ultimately deploy routines automatically without thinking too hard — much as we do with various elements of driving a car. This frees up working memory allowing us to attend to more dynamic elements of a lesson.

However, when working on new routines, such as **Cold Calling** or **Think, Pair, Share,** the steps can be clunky and awkward at first. This is entirely normal. Over time, with some feedback, the steps smooth out into a more fluid routine. Fluency can also develop in how techniques are sequenced — e.g. from **Signal, Pause, Insist** to **Show-Me Boards**.

BUILDING MENTAL MODELS | S|T|A|R|T

Inside our heads, we have deeply personal ideas about how the world works. These causal mental models shape how we act. For teachers, strong mental models allow for quick, informed decision-making, helping them assess, predict and respond to the changeability of the classroom. Mental models are the organising structures of the professional mind — coaching should develop them to support more intentional, responsive teaching.

The S|T|A|R|T framework codifies this process. Each stage is connected by a single causal thread, from identifying the problem to testing a prediction and drawing learning from the outcome.

1

SITUATION

Problems are an inherent part of teaching, for all teachers. Professionals seek them out. Building situational awareness is a core aim of coaching — developing the teacher's ability to notice what's happening, interpret it and define the problem clearly.

This means digging beneath surface behaviours to pinpoint underlying causes — e.g. recognising when students aren't focusing attention because transitions are unclear, or when low participation ratio stems from a poorly worded question. It's the clarity of this early analysis that shapes everything that follows.

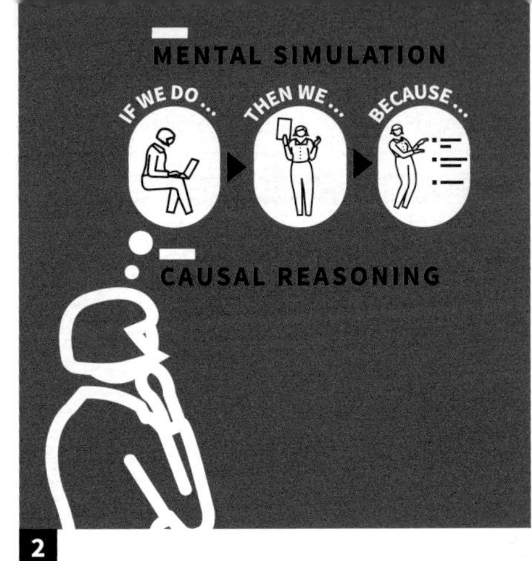

2

THEORY

Teachers constantly make rapid decisions about what will work and why. They run countless mental simulations of what might happen next, testing out different options and techniques, and choosing the most promising route.

Coaching brings this causal reasoning to the surface. Together, coach and teacher clarify the logic: if we do this, then we expect that — because...

This turns hunches into predictions, ready to be tested in action.

3

ACTIONS

The real test of a mental model is how well it supports action. Teachers apply their thinking in real time — adapting when needed, while keeping their core intention intact. Once a course of action is chosen, it must be enacted deliberately and precisely. For example, if a teacher decides to use **Cold Calling** to get every student thinking hard, they need to run the steps accurately: ask a question for the whole class, give thinking time and strategically select students to share their responses.

It's the visible outcome of prior thinking.

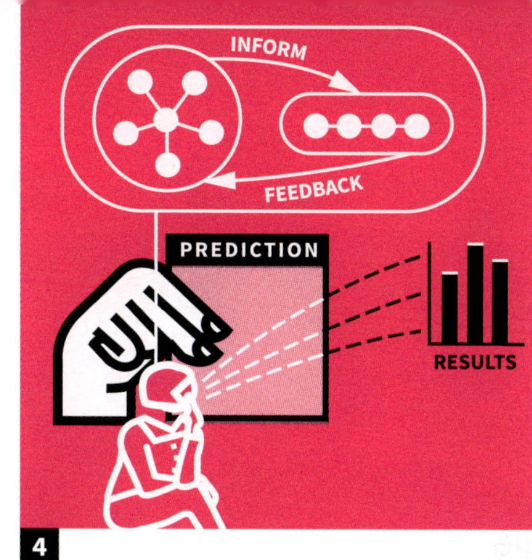

4

RESULTS

Mental models and schema work in a loop. Schema provides the foundation for mental models — but enacting them feeds back into and sharpens the schema.

Coaching supports the teacher to review outcomes through the lens of their prediction. Did the actions lead to the intended effects? If not, why not? What did we learn about the problem, and about the original theory?

Results are judged through evidence appropriate to the problem — the better the fit, the stronger the learning.

5

TAKEAWAYS

This final step is where learning crystalises. What's worth repeating, adjusting or dropping?

The teacher now compares their predicted outcomes to what actually happened, looking for alignment or error. Where was the reasoning sound? Where did it need refining? This is where mental models are strengthened — by refining cause and effect.

Team coaching can amplify this further. Shared insights, practical recommendations and honest reflections help everyone test and strengthen their thinking.

COACHING FOR INTENTIONALITY

Meaningful coaching requires a clear reference point: a shared vision of high-quality teaching. Without this, coaching can become vague and disconnected from real classroom needs. Coaching should help teachers move towards intentionality, enabling them to deliberately create the right conditions for learning. Here, we outline the characteristics of highly intentional teachers: those who act with purpose, apply techniques with precision and follow through.

Use this framework to guide coaching towards intentional, responsive and inclusive teaching.

1

PURPOSE

Teach with purpose. Every action should serve a clear goal. Choose the right approach at the right time — not out of habit, but because it fits the moment. For example:

- To get the whole class's attention, I'll use **Signal, Pause, Insist**.
- To get a quick hit of what all students are thinking, I'll use **Show-Me Boards**.
- To allow all students to rehearse their explanations with a partner, I'll use **Think, Pair, Share**.

2

PRECISION

Once the goal is clear, run the routine with accuracy. Every technique should be sharp, deliberate and consistent. For example, for **Signal, Pause, Insist**, stand at the front and give an assertive signal — don't mumble from behind your desk. For **Show-Me Boards**, expect a simultaneous reveal of whiteboards, not a hesitant trickle. Before you run a **Think, Pair, Share**, check that all students have a talk-partner, understand the task and have the knowledge to think deeply. Imprecise execution weakens impact.

AWARENESS

Coaching should support teachers to develop their professional vision. This means that they are close enough to the action to monitor student responses in real time.

Is everybody involved? Is everybody thinking? Take action if needed. Circulate the room, scanning to get a clear sense of what's happening in front of you — what students are doing and how successful they are. Pay close attention to what you see. If it's not working as intended, reorient and reset.

4

COMMITMENT

Now follow through. If a routine matters, see it through to the end — don't settle for half measures.

For example, in **Cold Call**, don't stop at one response. Ensure everyone is thinking. With **Show-Me Boards**, insist on a full-class reveal. Every board up, every time.

You've set the purpose — now make it happen. High expectations only work if you stick to them.

5

FLUENCY

Fluency comes from adapting in the moment. Combine techniques to respond to students in real time. For example:

- Blend **Cold Call** and **Think, Pair, Share** to form the foundation of dynamic whole class discussion.
- Adapt your **Show-Me Board** routine to using a digital survey tool.
- Build on a **Live Modelling** routine with **Think, Pair, Share** and **Practise Explaining**.

Intentional teaching isn't rigid. Blend, adapt and build on what you see.

CASE-BASED REASONING

Case-based reasoning is no more than an intuitive, everyday approach to problem- solving: using past solutions to solve current, similar problems. The assumption being that situations recur with regularity, and so by comparing past solutions with current challenges, we more easily find satisfactory answers.

Developed among doctors, its focus on problem-solving provides a highly appropriate model for coaching teachers. Its strength lies in its emphasis on the problem and not an evaluation of the individual. And its productivity stems from the use of collective memories, not just individual ones.

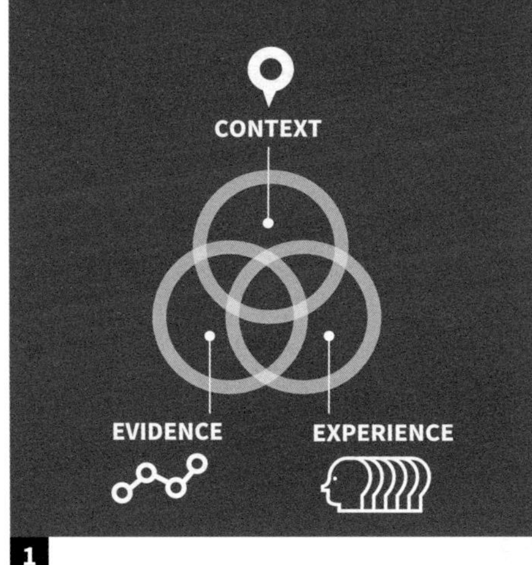

1

REASON IN ALL THREE DOMAINS

Medical practitioners don't follow clinical evidence unthinkingly. The context (patient and condition) is of paramount importance. They consider the balance of three domains.

CONTEXT | Just as links between patients, their characteristics and illness are considered, so too are the links between students, their learning and curriculum.

EVIDENCE | Professionals inform themselves of any and all related research.

EXPERIENCE | Maybe surprisingly, doctors use both personal and collective memory to deepen and accelerate reaching a solution. Teachers' experiences are similarly valuable; even more so as a collective memory bank.

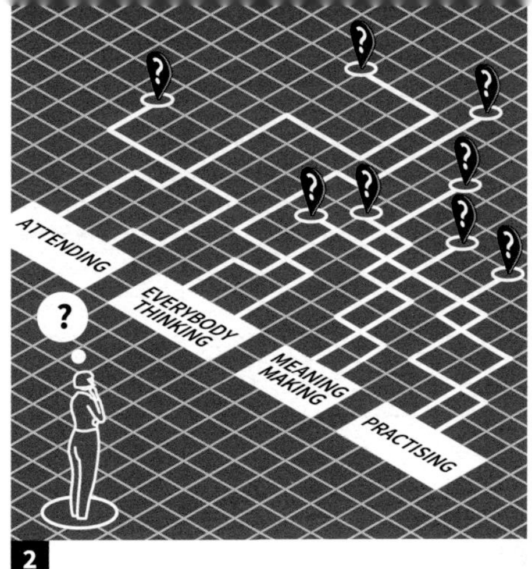

2

IDENTIFY YOUR SITUATION

As warns Viviane Robinson, it's critical to understand, at some depth, the nature of the problem being addressed. The danger of not doing so is a too-rapid search for solutions. Unless the situation is accurately identified, the search for solutions will be insufficiently informed and superficial. The challenge of time can be reduced by being systematic.

CHALLENGE PROBLEMS
BEHAVIOUR PROBLEMS
KNOWLEDGE PROBLEMS
PARTICIPATION PROBLEMS
FEEDBACK PROBLEMS

COMMON PROBLEMS

HOW DO I GET ALL STUDENTS' ATTENTION?
HOW DO I INVOLVE ALL STUDENTS IN QUESTIONING?
HOW DO I GET ALL STUDENTS THINKING HARD?
HOW DO I STRUCTURE PAIRED & GROUP TALK?
HOW DO I EXPLAIN IDEAS EFFECTIVELY? --------→
HOW DO I MODEL KEY CONCEPTS & PROCESSES?
HOW DO I CHALLENGE ALL STUDENTS APPROPRIATELY?
HOW DO I CHECK WHAT THEY KNOW?
HOW DO I TEACH MIXED-ATTAINING GROUPS?
HOW DO I MAKE RETRIEVAL PRACTICE EFFECTIVE?

3

MATCH & COMPARE YOUR SITUATION TO A PREVIOUS CASE

The WalkThrus have a Problem-Solution bank that serves as a collective memory of teachers' tried-and-tested teaching strategies.

Problems common to all teachers at some stage are easily identified.

Coaches can use this opportunity to explore the teacher's thinking around the features of their own problem and the one being matched. Zoom in on the similarities and differences. Ask the teacher for a narrative around the root causes to help develop their perception and thinking.

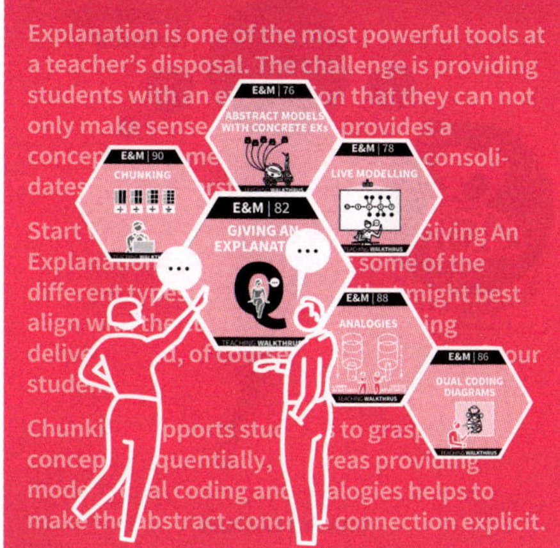

4

MAKE ADAPTATIONS

Arising from such a discussion is the opportunity to customise the solution of the memory bank of related cases. While there are many ways to do this, we find the structure of the A|D|A|P|T method creates an efficient familiarity with the process. Whatever the model, this is a practical opportunity to probe and explore the teacher's thinking.

If one acknowledges — as one must — the cognitive nature of teaching, then conversations about teaching must be about the cognition.

5

TRIAL & CONSIDER ARCHIVING THE ADAPTED CASE

With the results of your trial at hand, judge whether your adaptation is sufficiently different to warrant being considered a new solution.

If that's the case, then talk to the curators of whatever collection of cases you are using and offer yours as an addition. Spend some time with them in accurately labelling (indexing) your *play* (sequence of techniques) to enable others to readily identify it and relate it to their current problem.

KENNEDY'S PROBLEM OF ENACTMENT

It's common for teachers to leave training sessions full of ideas, but when reality hits, those ideas are easily forgotten. Kennedy (2016a) calls this the Problem of Enactment — more commonly known as the knowing-doing gap. Teachers can understand and value a new technique but still default to old routines when teaching. This isn't just resistance. It's about habit, uncertainty and making split-second decisions under pressure. This WalkThru explores the Problem of Enactment and the implications for coaches and leaders.

MARY KENNEDY

1

INITIAL FRAMES OF REFERENCE

All teachers arrive to the profession with an *apprenticeship of observation*. Their early school experiences as students form initial frames of reference; deeply held views about what teaching looks like. These frames shape how they interpret new ideas. If a new approach doesn't align with those frames, it's unlikely to stick, and teachers will default to their habitual practice.

Help the teacher surface and unpick their existing frame of reference to shift how they see the classroom.

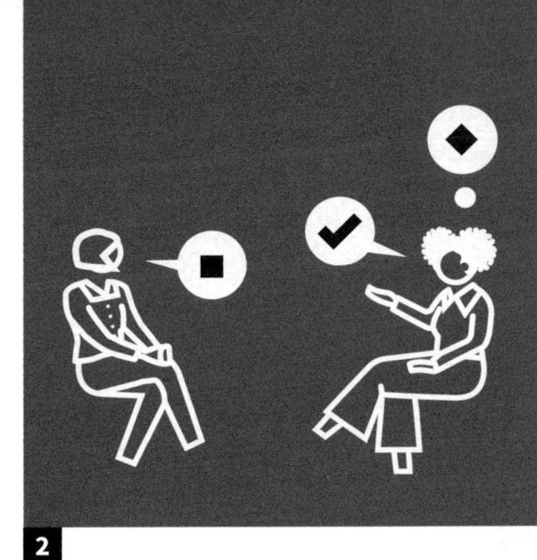

2

AMBIGUITY OF EDUCATIONAL LANGUAGE

Common pedagogical terms are often interpreted through the lens of a teacher's existing practice. This can lead to superficial or contradictory enactments that miss the core of the intended technique. Without a shared understanding, even well-meaning efforts fall flat. The WalkThrus toolkit helps address this ambiguity by providing a clear, consistent language for teaching and coaching.

Focus coaching conversations directly onto the WalkThru steps. This anchors the conversation in a shared language and reduces the risk of drift or misalignment.

3

ESPOUSED BELIEFS vs ENACTED PRACTICES

A teacher might believe they're using a new technique, but in the moment, familiar habits can take over and shape what actually happens. For example, a teacher may believe they are **Cold Calling** but in practice they continue to select students at random — because that's what they've always done. What teachers say they're doing and what they actually do can drift apart.

Help teachers examine the gap between how they think they're using a technique and what's actually happening in the room.

4

KNOWING WHEN TO ENACT NEW IDEAS

Even if teachers understand a technique, they may not see when might be the right time to use it. Teachers often try to use a technique because they want to get it right, but without a clear sense of when and why, it ends up feeling forced or misplaced. This is the knowing-doing gap in action: teachers know the technique but aren't confident in spotting the right moment to enact it.

Training is key — explore lots of examples, multiple models, boundary conditions and common misconceptions to sharpen decision-making.

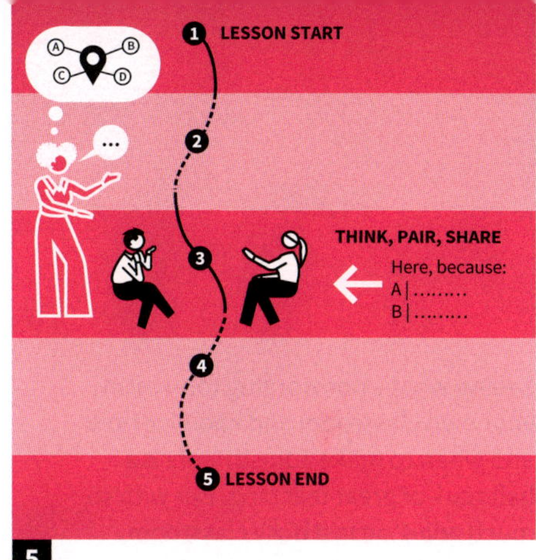

5

SITUATED KNOWLEDGE

Without situated knowledge — knowing how to apply an idea in different situations — a technique remains detached from classroom reality. For example, knowing when to use **Think, Pair, Share** to:

- Unpick misconceptions that emerge after a **Show-Me Board** check.
- Rehearse explanations of a tricky maths calculation.
- Explore prior knowledge at the start of a new topic.

Use rehearsal to build confidence in when and how to apply the technique.

GOODWIN'S PROFESSIONAL VISION

Seeing what's not working too well in your own classroom and knowing how and when to make adjustments is a hallmark of great teaching. But with so much going on in a busy classroom, this isn't an easy thing to do. This is where coaches can make a real difference to teachers.

Helping teachers to notice and make sense of what they see in the classroom — building what Charles Goodwin describes as professional vision — is an important part of the cognitive element of meaningful coaching.

CHARLES GOODWIN

MEANINGFUL COACHING 12 | PD MECHANISMS | WHY COACHING WORKS 14 | THE LEARNING MODEL | STUDENTS 16 | THE LEARNING MODEL | TEACHERS 18 | BUILDING MENTAL MODELS | S|T|A|R|T 20 | COACHING FOR INTENTIONALITY 22 | CASE-BASED REASONING 24 | KENNEDY'S PROBLEM OF ENACTMENT 26 | **GOODWIN'S PROFESSIONAL VISION 28** | GROSSMAN et al's REPRESENTATION, DECOMPOSITION & APPROXIMATION 30 |

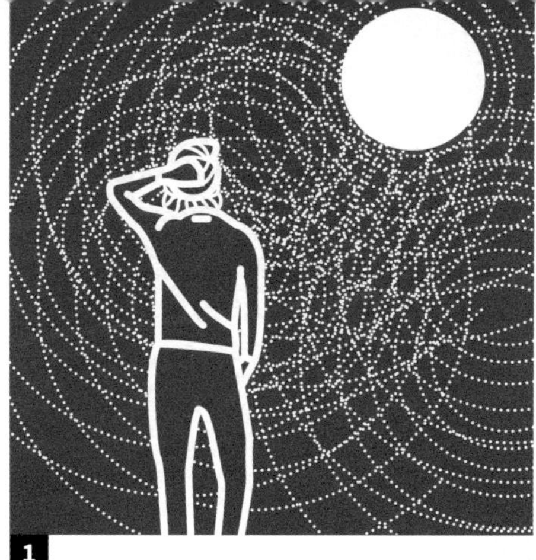

1

CUT THROUGH COMPLEXITY

Because classrooms are often such busy places, our view of how well students are learning can easily become congested. This makes it difficult to always notice and interpret the key moments in a lesson.

Cut through complexity by homing in on specific features. Instead of trying to take in a whole lesson, look more closely at smaller chunks — e.g. a single exchange or a WalkThru — that can be broken down and analysed in a productive and cohesive way.

2

BUILD MEANING TOGETHER

In order for both the teacher and the coach to contribute to the development of knowledge, make coaching a collaborative endeavour where meaning and action are co-constructed.

Take a dialogical approach to coaching conversations so that teachers not only feel involved, but also so that they recognise the problems that they are trying to solve. Try to pair this with a **Three-Point Communication** dynamic.

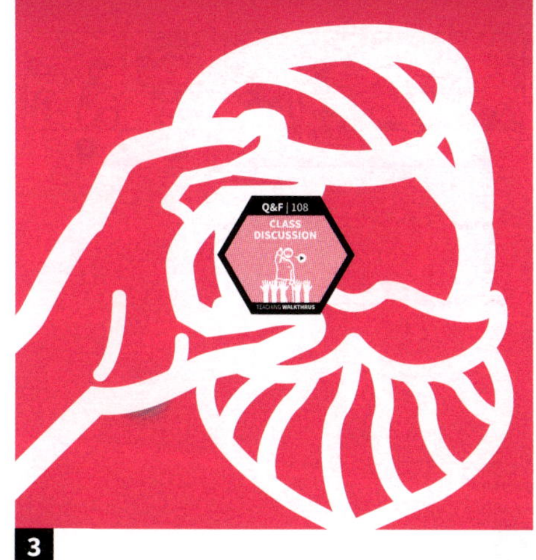

3 LOOK THROUGH A LENS

Just as archaeologists use colour charts to help them study different types of soil, coaches and teachers can use coding schemes to help them make sense of what they see happening in the classroom. It's helpful to look at learning through different lenses.

For example, use **The Learning Model** as a broad lens through which to identify and discuss common learning problems. Or use the five steps of a WalkThru as a narrow lens through which to discuss steps in a specific technique.

4 HIGHLIGHT KEY MOMENTS

While teaching a lesson, it's near impossible for a teacher to see everything that happens in front of them.

Offer an extra pair of eyes and point out important things that might have otherwise lay unseen in the busyness of the classroom. Use objective description and questions to build clarity and insight. Highlight important moments, bringing them into focus so that they can be properly discussed and scrutinised.

5 USE DIAGRAMS & VIDEOS

Sometimes words alone can't capture what's going on. That's when material representations, such as diagrams or videos, can help.

Map out classroom practice in graphical form to make nuanced ideas more accessible for analysis and reflection. Use the visual design of a WalkThru to help. Explore alternative approaches to modelling too, such as scripting, mental rehearsal and co-teaching.

GROSSMAN et al's REPRESENTATION, DECOMPOSITION & APPROXIMATION

Pam Grossman's research into professional learning has shaped how we think about developing expertise in teaching.

Her seminal paper *Teaching Practice: A Cross-Professional Perspective* (2009) highlights three key professional pedagogies that support teachers to transfer new ideas from the training room to the classroom: representation, decomposition and approximation. This WalkThru explores the implications for coaches.

PAM GROSSMAN

1 REPRESENTATION

Representations of practice make teaching visible through modelling. They help teachers observe key moves and decisions, and understand how techniques might work in real life. Use models that show the technique in action and allow scrutiny of reasoning and decision-making, building understanding of what's happening and why it matters.

Use our **Principles of Modelling** alongside the approaches in **Ways of Modelling** to embed high-quality representations into the coaching process.

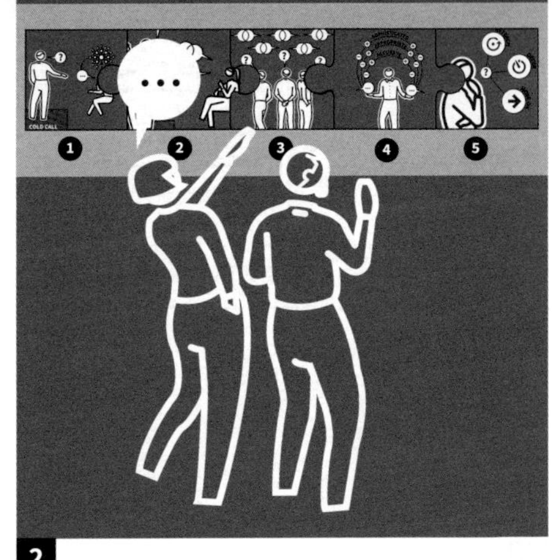

2 DECOMPOSITION

Decomposition breaks ideas about teaching down into their component parts, so that teachers and coaches can scrutinise the grammar of practice. This is why the format of our WalkThru techniques works so well — without clear parts, understanding drifts and practice stays vague.

Naming the parts — building a shared understanding of the core ingredients — means techniques can be worked on in a cohesive way.

Use the steps in **Name It | Decomposition, Recomposition** to help.

3

APPROXIMATION

Teachers need time to test out new techniques before they hit the classroom. Running approximations — rehearsal — in a low-stakes training room setting provides opportunities for feedback and fine-tuning, as well as building familiarity and confidence. The key is that approximations are as authentic as possible — framed through real classrooms and curriculum.

This can be done in different ways — see **Training Room Rehearsal** for ideas.

4

INTEGRATION

Representations, decomposition and approximations aren't isolated pedagogies; they overlap and reinforce each other.

Recomposition is the process of connecting the pieces — the models, the steps and the rehearsal — and applying them in real classrooms.

Help the teacher integrate and apply what they've seen, named and practised. Use the **A|D|A|P|T** process to shape the technique to their context so it fits their lesson, subject and students.

5

REVISIT AS PART OF ONGOING SUPPORT

These are not linear stages — they're tools to revisit as part of the ongoing practical support coaches provide to teachers.

Within a coaching cycle, you'll naturally return to these approaches when needed — this is part of being flexible as a coach. You might need to review a model, rename the parts or rehearse a tricky element again. The key is continued support that follows through to full implementation.

WALKTHRU SECTIONS

HOW?

Coaching can only make an impact when it is well designed and built into the everyday work of schools. The How? section outlines key design decisions, structures and processes that make coaching realistic and sustainable. It draws on lessons from our work with schools and colleges and provides clear implementation guidance for leaders, coaches and teachers. A key tool here is our WalkThrus PDM Model — Prepare It, Design It, Make It Happen — which we see as the ideal starting point.

THE WALKTHRUs COACHING PROCESS

The WalkThrus Coaching Process is an iterative process designed to build knowledge, motivate staff, develop teaching techniques and embed practice. Each phase builds on the last, supporting a realistic and sustainable approach to developing teachers individually or in teams. The core headings of the book form this framework, pulling everything together. The aim is to enact **Meaningful Coaching**, balancing the personal, cognitive and technical dimensions of professional development while making the most of our Teaching WalkThrus toolkit. It's a flexible process, not a rigid model, capturing the spirit of respectful, collaborative coaching.

1

DIAGNOSE & DESIGN

Start by diagnosing the problem. Whether individual, team or whole-school, challenges must be based on real observations of where students are struggling. Use lesson visits, student data and video to gather insights. Lean into research on how learning happens and why it sometimes fails. Analyse learning problems, identify cause-and-effect patterns and test hunches before deciding on the best way forward. Once the issue is clear, explore multiple solutions before selecting a single WalkThru technique as a starting point. Then, design a goal that links purpose to action.

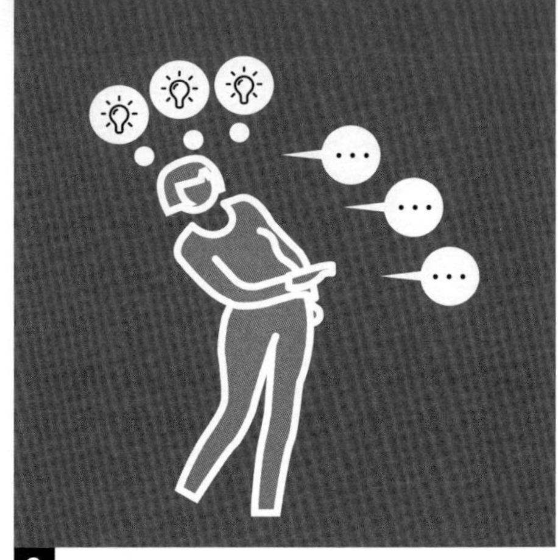

2

TRAIN & MODEL

The next step is to ensure teachers understand why and how the technique works — and when it might not. A great training workshop builds teachers' schema and develops their mental models for teaching. We recommend our adaptation of Bambrick-Santoyo's **Theory, See It, Name It, Do It** as a training framework. Unpack the theory behind the approach, then deconstruct models, scenarios, examples and non-examples to build secure understanding. Break the technique down step by step, naming its key components, and rehearse with feedback before taking it into the classroom.

3

ADAPT & APPLY

WalkThrus are context-free by design — they become effective when shaped to fit a teacher's classroom and curriculum. This can take time, space and support from a coach. Our A|D|A|P|T framework helps teachers personalise the technique, ensuring it fits their specific context. Practising in real conditions with cues, prompts and checklists supports teachers to embed the technique with intentionality and fluency. Coaches should provide ongoing practical and social support during this phase, running reality checks in good faith, designed to build insight and collect helpful information ready to share with the teacher.

4

FEEDBACK & SUPPORT

Coaching conversations, whether one-to-one or in teams, help teachers reflect, see progress and plan next steps. These are the pivotal moments where the coach is most responsive, flexing along the coaching continuum and between modes. Stay close to the teaching and learning focus, using **The 5Ps Framework** to affirm what's working, uncover what hasn't landed, diagnose sticking points and construct next steps. Manage dialogue to deepen and mediate thinking, asking questions that build clarity, insight and action. The spirit here is a shared commitment to a breakthrough, not shallow conversations that lead nowhere.

5

EMBED & BUILD

It takes a long time to build new habits and even longer to change old ones. The ultimate goal is for teachers to intentionally apply techniques at the right time for the right purpose. Support them through the stages of learning, using prompts, cues and checklists to stamp in changes and ensure techniques are fully embedded. Recognise and celebrate success, amplifying what has real impact for students, but don't stop there. Use our Clustering concept to connect new techniques that build on the improved practice. Iterate, develop and improve.

PREPARE IT

One of the strongest findings from our field experience working with schools is that it's very powerful for school leaders to do some groundwork before rushing to design and implement a full-blown professional learning and coaching programme. Time spent in the **Prepare It** phase will be very worthwhile in the long run.

A pilot programme is an excellent idea for most settings, allowing leaders to test their thinking with a small group of people before launching with everyone, maximising the chances of it being a success.

1

THE KEY CONCEPTS

There is a lot of literature regarding learning for students and teachers. We recommend as a start that leaders engage with:

- **The Learning Model** (Book 2) understanding how children learn and the barriers they encounter.
- The key ideas from Rosenshine, Willingham and Wiliam (Book 1).
- Mechanisms of Effective PD to understand how coaching supports them all (Book 3).
- The Why? section in this book to give you a firm basis for the rationale for your programme design.

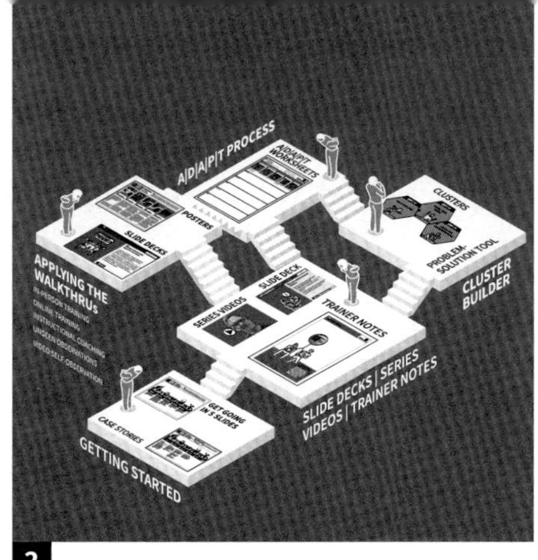

2

THE WALKTHRUs TOOLKIT

While it's powerful to focus on just a few WalkThrus techniques at any one time, we recommend that leaders have a good overview of the content of the toolkit to support future planning and responses to specific problems.

Create time and space to build confidence and familiarity with the WalkThrus toolkit and the way the content is organised, running sessions to browse the books or the members' site, involving all members of staff. The quick-start guides and problem-solution toolkit on the website help you to get stuck into the detailed content.

3

YOUR CURRENT REALITY & GOALS

Before making changes, make sure you know your current reality:

- What is the current quality of learning?
- Where are the main challenges?
- What systems are currently in place, and are they working?
- Who are your key drivers of change in the school and in each team?
- Who will need support to add to your leadership and coaching capacity?

Think hard about your key priorities and the systems that will deliver them. Create goals to shape your thinking at whole-school, team and individual levels.

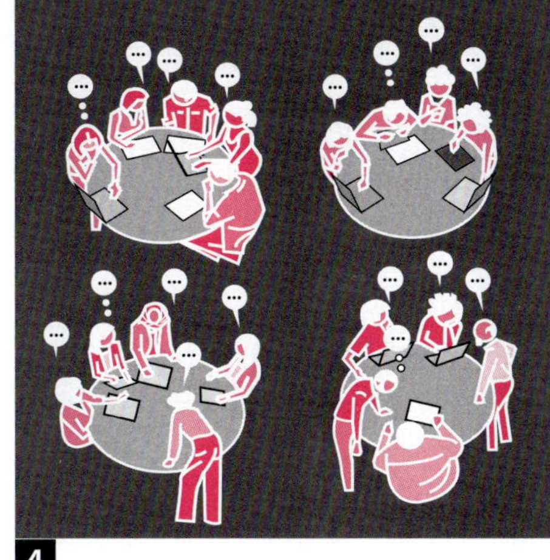

4

THE LAUNCH

Plan and deliver a whole-staff launch, making sure everyone is involved!

Explore the context and rationale behind the WalkThrus, thinking hard about learning and why students struggle.

Demonstrate a couple of core techniques so that teachers actually experience the techniques and see how a WalkThru works as a tool.

Avoid presenting WalkThrus as extra, different or radically new. Show that the tools are just a way of supporting your existing work and thinking, sharpening the focus on tried-and-tested ideas.

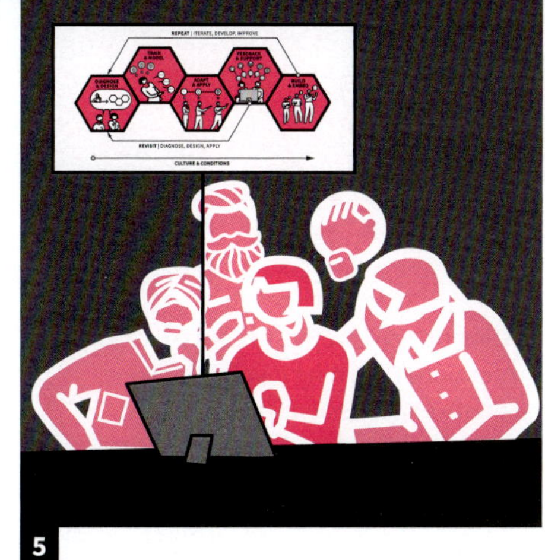

5

RUNNING YOUR PILOT

Run a pilot with a core group to help you to prototype your model. Include a coaching cycle and some feedback conversations. Use **Design It** to help you plan but limit the number of people or teams involved at first, or run the process for a short period of time.

We recommend selecting a universal focus that everyone can find value in, like **Cold Call** or **Think, Pair, Share.** Test your system to see what works and what doesn't. Evaluate the pilot to see where changes to the system might be needed — e.g. how long cycles run and when in the week the coaching will take place.

DESIGN IT

Setting up an effective process for professional learning involves making each of our *Six Design Decisions*. We explore these in detail on our website. We arrived at our codified structure after several years of fieldwork where we found we were routinely exploring each area with school leaders.

It pays to consider each decision in turn, starting with an analysis of the current position and then planning any changes that are needed for the next term or year. Significantly, it's normal and healthy for schools to start off with a set of initial decisions that then change in response to growing capacity for coaching and understanding of the techniques.

1

THE TEAMS, THE PEOPLE

Based on the capacity in your school, which units of people will deliver the best outcomes in your context?

- A specialist team of coaches, each coaching multiple teachers?
- Pairs of teachers, trained to coach each other?
- Pairs of teachers, each coached by a coach or leader?
- Triads or small groups of teachers working together?
- Existing subject teams or year/phase teams, either coached by their leader or a specialist coach?

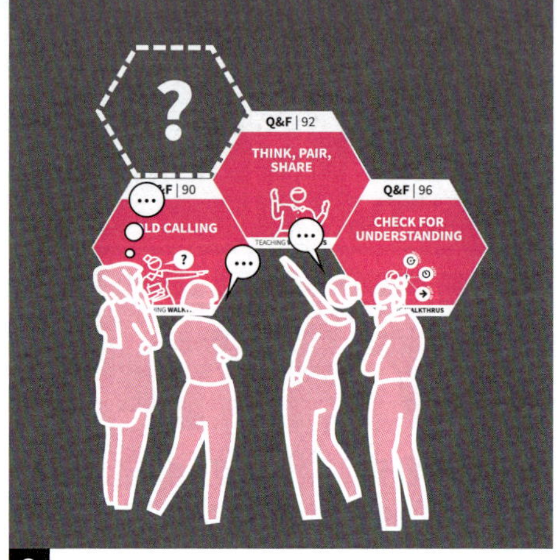

2

THE TEACHING & LEARNING FOCUS

Based on your analysis of the key learning problems, across the school or within specific teams, which cluster of techniques will offer the best set of solutions? Use the Problem-Solution and Cluster-Builder tools to help make the selection.

We often find the best progress is made by focusing on 3-5 core techniques in the first year, just to get them firmly embedded. Look at the **Tennis Player Analogy** — you are choosing core techniques that everyone uses with a high frequency. That then provides a platform for further exploration.

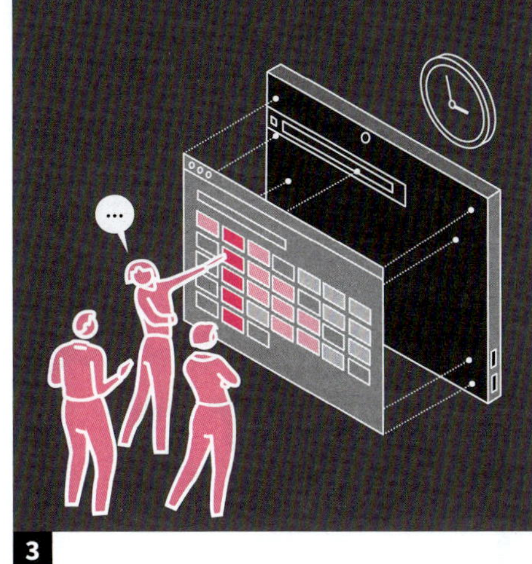

3

TIME STRUCTURE & TRAINING INPUTS

Decisions 3 and 4 come together here in planning the calendar for the year.

Aim to have coaching or team sessions every 2-4 weeks across the year. This might end up as 10-15 sessions that call you to construct multiple coaching cycles, plan actions and review progress.

Plan each teacher and each coach's allocation of time for learning walks, observations and feedback conversations.

Alongside, plan the training inputs, timing them to match the WalkThrus focus for the subsequent cycles.

4

THE COACHING PROCESS

Commit to a codified coaching process that you train everyone to use. As you'll become aware reading this book, our preferred model is the Paul Bambrick-Santoyo **5Ps** coaching protocol. This works well with groups of all sizes and supports focused feedback around WalkThrus steps.

However, there are alternatives. The key is that everyone knows what process you will use and this informs lesson observations, any documents and the spirit of each coaching interaction.

Plan training for everyone involved so the protocol is widely understood.

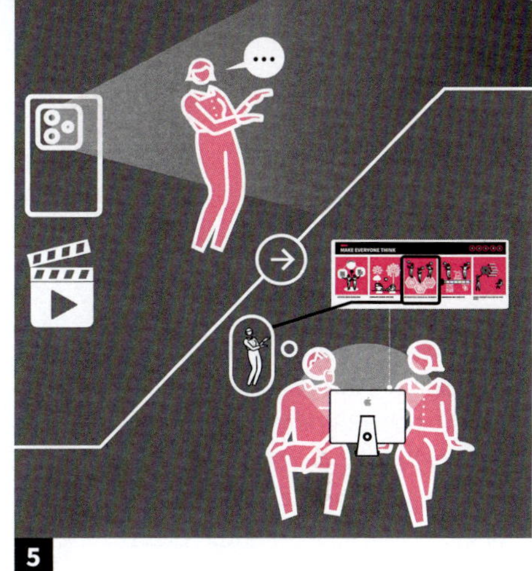

5

THE REALITY CHECK PROCESS

Estabish a well-defined set of processes that allow teachers to gain some meaningful feedback about their practice in such a way that it supports their development. This might include a combination of:

- Planned coach observations, focused on action steps agreed in the coaching session.
- Learning walks by team leaders, feeding into each subsequent team coaching meeting.
- Video observation — shared by teacher with coach or leader.
- Planned peer observation.

MAKE IT HAPPEN

We find that, despite good design intentions, it's not uncommon for the reality to turn out differently. Common issues include:

- After a launch, the system loses energy; coaching meetings don't happen.
- There is patchy engagement; some teams or teachers are fully involved while others are not.
- There's a lot of activity that isn't actually improving standards of teaching.
- There's a lack of precision in using steps within the WalkThrus.

It's vital to make it happen, embedding new systems and deep coaching culture.

1

DELIVER THE TRAINING

As we set out in the **Train & Model** series, coaching thrives when it feeds off strong training inputs that ensure everyone knows what techniques look like and how they address learning problems teachers experience.

Invest time in planning strong, interactive training sessions, using **Theory, See It, Name It, Do It**. Give teachers time to discuss their ideas and concerns. Make training on WalkThrus a big feature of the CPD programme. This will support all the coaching that will follow.

2

RUN THE CYCLES

Make sure all meetings needed for a complete coaching cycle can and do happen. Remove barriers so these vital sessions cannot be cancelled. Make sure everyone knows the dates and that the meetings are going on across the school, creating a sense of collective endeavour.

Be forensic in making sure teachers' and coaches' timetables allow them time for meeting each other: built-in, not merely hoped for. Use simple tracking tools to ensure planned meetings do actually take place and intervene if they fall away for any reason.

3

RUN REALITY CHECKS

A key component in these processes having an impact is that leaders and coaches are close to the teaching that actually happens — they must see through planned reality checks:

- Learning walks are absolutely routine and low stakes.
- Peer observations are carried out according to a plan.
- Coaches always see a lesson or a video prior to a session.
- Create a culture where nobody turns up to sessions without having completed the reality checks they committed to.

4

REVIEW TEACHING & LEARNING

After a few months of activity and then on an ongoing basis, it's crucial to evaluate whether all the coaching and training is having an impact. There will be a mixed picture with some people making great strides and others less so.

- Evaluate whether the coaching process needs to develop more strongly — coaches and leaders may need more training.
- Evaluate whether the selection of techniques matches the needs of learners closely enough.
- Make any changes necessary.

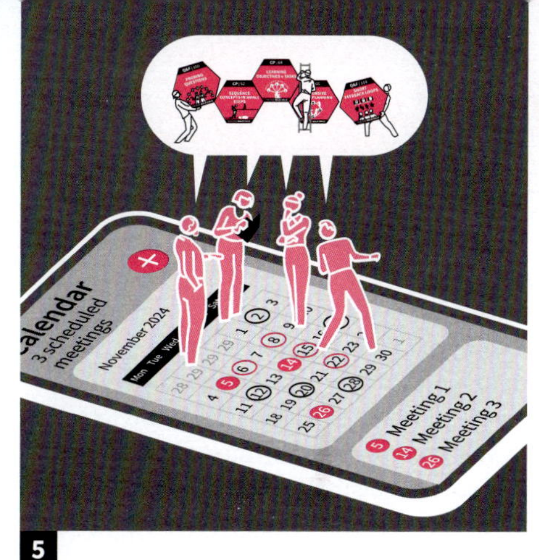

5

REVIEW THE SYSTEM

Evaluate whether the details of the system are working:

- Do you have people in the most effective combinations or teams?
- Do you have too many WalkThrus on the go, perhaps where training wasn't carried out?
- Is the time frequency intense enough? Are you using the best time slot in the week to sustain the coaching cycles?
- Are formal observations still going on and getting in the way with mixed messages about accountability and developmental feedback?

THREE-STREAM CPD

It's important to regard coaching as just one part of a more extensive programme for delivering professional development. We advocate conceiving this as three distinct but interrelated streams:

- Whole school (or college).
- Teams (subjects, primary year teams).
- Individuals.

Each stream has an important role to play both in terms of fostering a culture that embraces professional learning and coaching and in terms of delivering technical inputs leading to positive change in student learning.

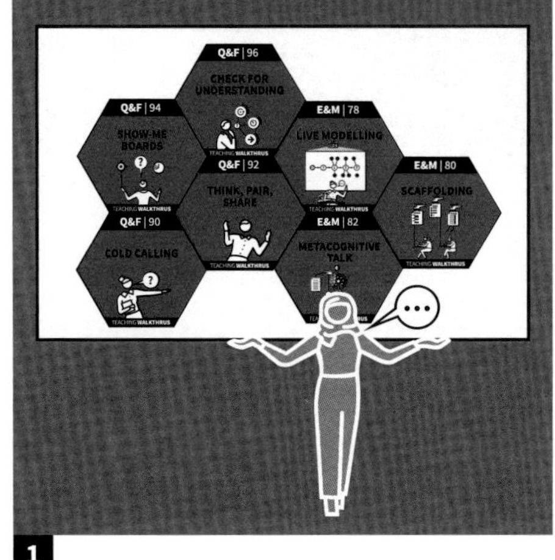

1

AGREE THE AGENDA

School CPD systems can be complex, made up of multiple elements — teachers, leaders, planning meetings, training sessions, lesson observations, coaches and feedback sessions.

For this array of activity across the three streams to have coherence, there needs to be a strong agenda to bind it all together. As part of the overall design, teachers should be involved in co-constructing and evaluating a whole-school framework for teaching. A core agenda then sets the direction; the common purpose around which everything should align.

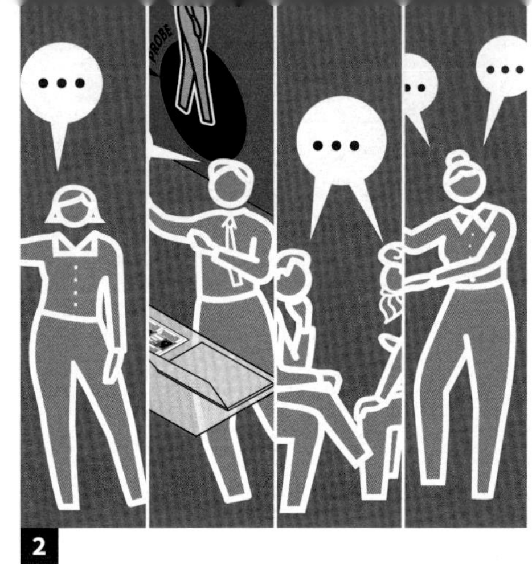

2

PLAN WHOLE-SCHOOL INPUTS

Decide which aspects of professional learning would be usefully delivered so that everyone engages with the same material and messages. Examples might include:

- Introductions to concepts about learning that apply to everyone, linked to some research.
- Training on coaching protocols.
- Discussions about curriculum concepts in maths across a primary school.
- Training on **Think, Pair, Share** with **Theory, See It, Name It, Do It**.

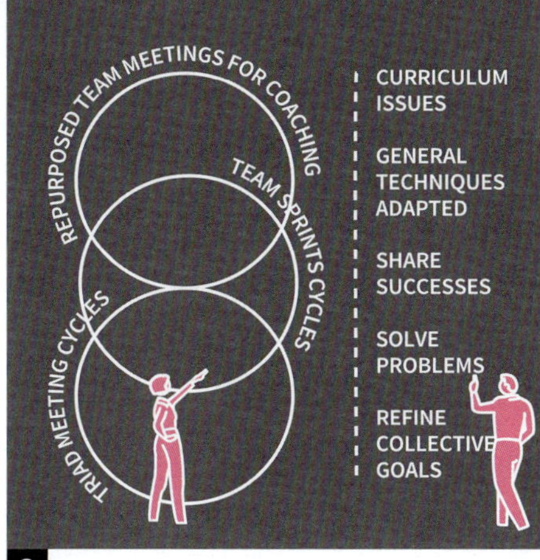

3

RUN TEAM CYCLES

Ideally, team meeting cycles that are planned into the calendar dovetail with whole-school inputs, including:

- Regular team meetings repurposed for team coaching.
- **Teaching Sprints** cycles.
- Triad meeting cycles.

Within team cycles, curriculum issues can be explored and general techniques adapted to support curriculum enactment. Teachers can share successes and problems to solve, using the 5Ps. Collective goals can be refined.

4

GENERATE INDIVIDUAL ACTIONS

Individual teachers might engage in one-to-one coaching cycles or coaching with a colleague.

Coaches should support a teacher to construct action steps to support them in working to the team's agreed agenda around curriculum and student outcomes. It's unhelpful if they see their own agenda as entirely separate or they risk being in conflict. However, individual support can always run alongside the team cycles in highly personal areas such as behaviour management or where they are struggling in a specific way.

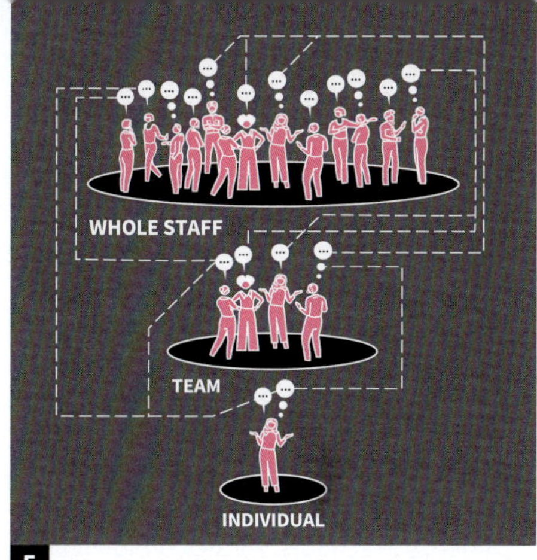

5

MAKE IT FLOW COHERENTLY

This concept could be perceived in a top-down manner with directives passed from senior leaders, to teams and then to teachers. However, the flow should go both ways.

Senior leaders should have a good sense of their staff's needs overall but the agenda should be informed continually by ideas shared by teachers within and between teams. If teacher input is high, the flow of ideas will be more likely to lead to changes in practice.

Strong alignment emerges through consensus and reinforcement, rather than directives and enforcement.

COACHING CONFIGURATIONS

There are some purist schools of thought that would define coaching exclusively as a one-to-one scenario.

However, based on our extensive experience in schools, we are confident that not only is it often necessary to coach teachers in pairs, threes, small groups or a whole staff body (often for practical reasons), but it is also highly effective and even preferable.

Often a mix of configurations can co-exist to good effect and it's helpful to plan on this basis.

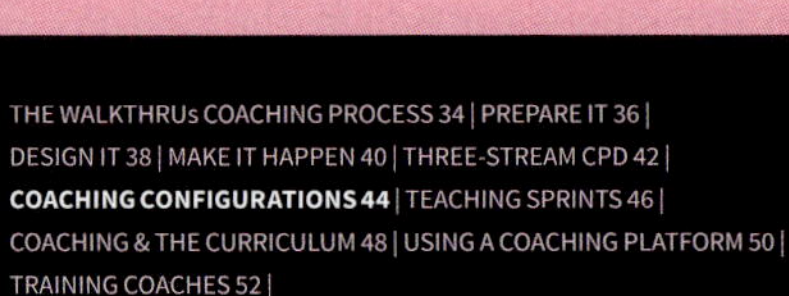

1

ONE-TO-ONE

COACH-TEACHER | Identify and train a team of specialist coaches who coach a number of teachers each. Coaching expertise across the team can be strong in this model, but time must be allocated to coaches to operate in this role.

PEER-TO-PEER COACHING | Pair teachers up to coach each other. This spreads coaching skills across a whole staff body but requires extensive training and scaffolding to ensure the coaching quality is high enough to have an impact.

2

COACHED PAIRS

Coaching two people at a time works extremely well when both teachers are in the same primary year team or teach the same subject.

The coaching conversations tend to focus on shared challenges within the shared curriculum and, because the dialogue is open, the conversations can continue beyond the coaching session. Being coached together fosters a sense of solidarity and encourages openness in discussing problems and difficulties. Pragmatically, this also halves the number of meetings needed making it more sustainable.

3

COACHING TRIADS

As with pairs, coaching in larger groups is possible but the larger the group, the more group dynamics need to be taken into account. With triads, our view is that it works better if someone in each triad is nominally the leader to ensure the protocols for the conversations are followed. The cycles of design, adapting and generating feedback need to run a few times so participants gain confidence with process of observation, feedback and action planning.

It can help for triads to report back to an external person periodically to share their journey and keep momentum.

4

COACHING IN TEAMS

In this set-up the team leader develops their role to act as a team coach alongside their other duties.

They would typically conduct routine learning walks, visiting all or most teachers between planned team sessions. In each session the **Team Conversations** process is used to ensure each teacher is engaged in the dialogue and constructs action steps in response to the reflection and feedback.

In teams, the link to curriculum design is strong and the momentum from collective action can be very powerful to drive change.

5

COACHING AS A WHOLE-STAFF TEAM

In some settings, the whole staff can act like one very large team where common problems are explored and feedback from observations is generated and discussed collectively.

If the meetings are just a few weeks apart, leaders have time to undertake observations through learning walks and can create iterative feedback loops like those in the other configurations. The sessions must give time for each teacher to translate the discussion and general feedback into specific actions, ideally with everyone making a record for reference in the next cycle.

TEACHING SPRINTS

As covered in *WalkThrus 2*, Teaching Sprints exemplify team-driven professional learning. Devised by Simon Breakspear and Bronwyn Ryrie Jones, Sprints support teachers to learn about, practise and review a small slice of their teaching over a short period of time.

The intensity of this collaborative process is a powerful catalyst, injecting energy and generating focused commitment from teachers to move their practice forward. The Teaching Sprints structure draws on many elements of team coaching and is an excellent vehicle for taking WalkThrus from the page to the classroom.

1

SET UP FOR SUCCESS

Before your team starts a Teaching Sprint, it's a good idea to map out the time and resources you'll need to move through the three phases — Prepare, Sprint, Review.

Make sure all the sessions you need are fully calendared and protected from other activities. The 2-4-week cycle brings intensity and immediate impact so this has to be planned for, perhaps by repurposing existing meetings, not by adding more. Team size can vary but it's vital that all teachers have a voice in group discussions.

2

PHASE 1 | PREPARE

In the Prepare Phase, your team gets clarity on an aspect of instruction you want to improve. This involves engaging with the *best bets* from the evidence base and agreeing on intended practice improvements. The Prepare Phase ends when all members of the team commit to practising a specific evidence-based technique or strategy in the Sprint Phase.

This could be one WalkThrus technique or step, or a small cluster. It's vital to establish absolute clarity about what the techniques will look like when practised with fidelity.

3

PHASE 2 | SPRINT

The Sprint Phase is all about bridging theory to practice; here, the mode of learning shifts to intentional practice. Over 2 to 4 weeks, each team member practises the agreed technique in their classrooms.

Throughout the Sprint, the team monitors the impact of new approaches, and teachers adapt the strategies based on impact on their students. Supported by a simple protocol, the group meets for a quick, focused check-in to monitor progress and sustain momentum.

The Attempt, Develop and Adapt elements of **A|D|A|P|T** come into play here.

4

PHASE 3 | REVIEW

After 2 to 4 weeks in the Sprint Phase, your team comes together again to close out the Teaching Sprint. During the Review Phase, you reflect on learning as practitioners.

The team discusses changes to practice, considers the impact evidence and decides how new learning might be transferred into future practice. Observation may play a roll here but Sprints can also be largely a supported self-review process.

It works well to use **The 5Ps Framework** process to structure the review.

5

THINK AHEAD

Forming new instructional habits is hard, and all professional learning takes time. At the end of the Sprint, teachers may want to continue refining implementation of the new instructional technique, entering another cycle — as in any coaching process. The team may equally decide to revisit the research literature, or think more deeply about the broader possibilities for further improvement in this area of instruction.

The Practise and Test elements of **A|D|A|P|T** come into play as teachers continue to embed the technique into their everyday habits.

COACHING & THE CURRICULUM

An inherent element of a teacher's knowledge base is the subject knowledge they are teaching including the content of the curriculum and the deeper knowlege that underpins it.

There is also their pedogogical content knowledge (PCK); the specialist knowledge of how to teach the curriculum, where different subject disciplines demand particular approaches. Knowledge of general teaching techniques like **Cold Calling** is intertwined with PCK. Strong coaching should engage with teachers' development needs in relation to the curriculum and PCK, without being limited to discussing generic issues.

1

INCLUDE CURRICULUM EXPLICITLY

As a consequence of many coaches working in a generalist capacity, where they don't teach the subject of their coachee, there's a risk that curriculum issues are not identified or not addressed. We would recommend that coaches explicitly seek to engage in curriculum issues as part of the coaching flow, perhaps referencing **Coaching Outside Specialism** if relevant. When observing lessons or discussing a teacher's sense of their challenges and goals, raise questions about the content. Be explicit in linking your conversations to those happening within the teacher's curriculum team.

2

DIAGNOSE THROUGH A CURRICULUM LENS

Explore common challenges and learning problems:

- The degree of difficulty of the material: do students' secure a success rate?
- The sequence of ideas as they accumulate: can students make sense of it, assimilating knowledge at an appropriate depth?
- The quality of outcomes: are students clear about the expected standards and are they meeting them?
- The quality of resources: is it sufficiently high to support all students' learning? Do they do enough reading?

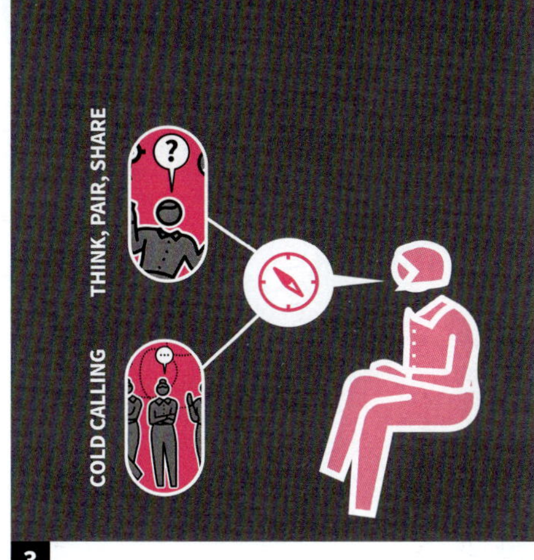

3

ADAPT AND APPLY WITH A CURRICULUM LENS

Here, the focus is exploring common ideas about instruction, making sure they're adapted appropriately to the subject:

- Which questions are being asked for **Cold Calling** or **Think, Pair, Share**?
- Are the responses appropriately challenging or probing?
- Is the modelling staged well so that the handover (I do, We do, You do) is effective?
- Are there appropriate scaffolds to support success?
- Is the nature of retrieval practice successful in relation to the material under review?

4

IDENTIFY COMMON TEAM ISSUES

Learning walks and coaching sessions with multiple teachers could show that they experience common challenges. Here, it could be more efficient to explore the issues collectively:

- Resources need adapting to improve the depth of learning or increase difficulty.
- The selection of questions in the planning needs more examples or better sequencing.
- A need for more exemplars at different standards to highlight success criteria.
- More work is needed to design scaffolds for certain learners.

5

TRAIN ON CURRICULUM SPECIFICS

Coaching has more impact if there has already been strong training input so teachers and coaches have a clear shared understanding of what success will look like. In a curriculum context, training on subject-specific elements of pedagogy is critical. For example, coaching on:

- Shared writing or delivering the phonics programme or a history topic.
- Running a science practical.
- Teaching a unit on a new English text.
- Running a PE training routine.
- Introducing an art technique.

USING A COACHING PLATFORM

Coaching is a powerful tool for improving teaching. But — like anything of real value — it's tough to get right. A platform can provide support by adding structure, sharing detailed content and providing useful insights around impact.

It's important to recognise, however, that the platform is a tool for, not the driver of, impact.

Here, the Steplab CEO Josh Goodrich discusses the benefits of using a platform to drive coaching, with Steplab providing a superb example of what is possible.

JOSH GOODRICH

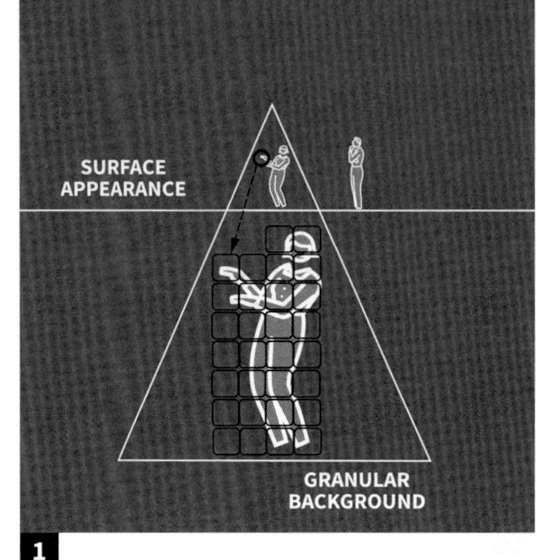

1

DIAGNOSE EFFECTIVELY

Coaching diagnosis is difficult. This is why I designed Steplab around a wealth of granular content to support it. Coaches begin by identifying fundamental learning problems: does a teacher need to focus on securing attention or optimising communication, for example? Coaches can then drill down, selecting specific, granular steps that teachers can implement immediately. Each step provides coaches with additional powerful content, such as success criteria, research and rehearsal tasks, just when they need it.

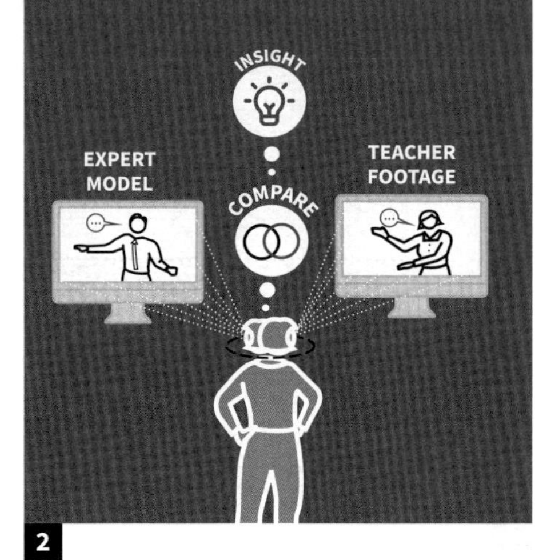

2

HARNESS THE POWER OF VIDEO

Models are essential ingredients for teacher development. Steplab includes a library of hundreds of expert video models. In addition, it enables coaches to combine these with footage shot in the teacher's own classroom.

Coaches can make video even more powerful through analysis tools that mark key moments, set focusing questions and highlight specific areas of the classroom to build teacher awareness.

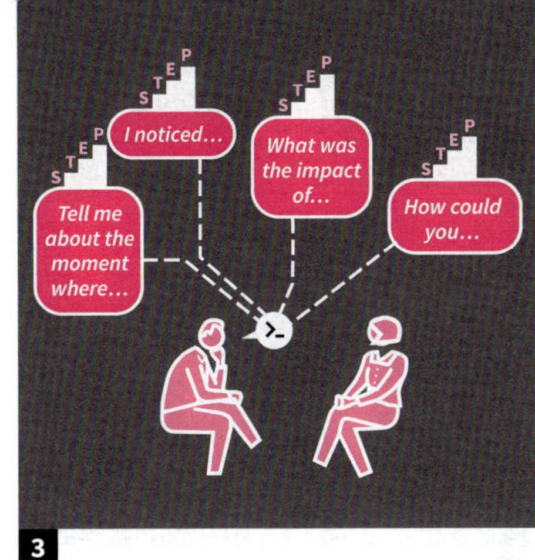

3

PLAN FEEDBACK CAREFULLY

Not all coaching is equal: it's a coach's job to plan for an impactful feedback conversation. Steplab provides carefully researched, adaptable coaching prompts. For example:

Tell me about the moment where…/ I noticed…/ What was the impact of…/ How could you…

This is a sure-fire recipe for guiding a teacher to agree a suitable next step. Additionally, each step comes with bespoke models, study and rehearsal tasks to scaffold great coaching conversations.

4

DRILL INTO DATA

Coaching programmes are extremely complex. Unless leaders are on top of what's happening, whether it's of high quality and whether it's working, it's easy for even the best programmes to run out of steam.

Steplab enables leaders to drill into the data, showing where teachers are focusing their attention, what's working and where further support is needed. Leaders can use this to spotlight good practice and adapt and plan strategic PD.

5

INTEGRATE COACHING WITH DROP-INS

Research tells us that teachers learn best in schools with a collegiate approach. On top of coaching, teachers should spend time dropping in to lessons and sharing best practice. There's a risk, however, that these drop-ins can become aimless.

A coaching platform prevents this by sharing important information about a teacher's learning history, current focus and any school development priorities, allowing visitors to carefully adapt their drop-in feedback for maximum benefit. Without a platform, this critical information is difficult to come by.

TRAINING COACHES

An obvious challenge for schools is turning teachers into coaches who have the knowledge and competence to fulfil the role effectively. It's not about promoting your best teachers into the role, nor is it a role reserved for the naturally gifted. Identify and train coaches who have the potential to do the job well.

Like teaching, coaching is something that can be learned. Leaders should provide a coaching curriculum to ensure coaches develop the right knowledge and competencies to be useful to teachers. In this WalkThru, we'll outline five core elements of a coaching curriculum.

1

KNOWLEDGE ABOUT HOW LEARNING HAPPENS

Train coaches in how learning happens — core concepts from **The Learning Model** — to build their capacity to support teachers in a research-informed way. Coaches must develop their own **Professional Vision** — learning to recognise the deep structure of the classroom, identify symptoms of learning problems and help teachers understand them. Ensure coaches engage with the most up-to-date findings from cognitive science, giving them time to read and discuss the implications for classroom practice.

The Why? chapters across our WalkThrus toolkit are a great place to start.

2

KNOWLEDGE OF EFFECTIVE TEACHING

Coaches need a broad understanding of key elements of effective teaching, starting with **Rosenshine's Principles of Instruction**. They need to build a deep understanding of explaining, modelling, questioning and retrieval, and to be able to describe and model techniques effectively. Coaches must understand what techniques are and aren't, their boundary conditions, misconceptions and how they can be adapted.

If WalkThrus is your playbook, ensure coaches are using the techniques in their own classrooms — they need to know them inside out!

3

KNOWLEDGE ABOUT COACHING

Coaches must learn how to coach. This is one of the core aims of this book. Being a great teacher doesn't automatically make someone a great coach. Coaches need to master key principles such as how to watch a lesson, run training workshops, rehearsal and feedback conversations. These areas should be part of a comprehensive coaching curriculum.

It's also crucial for both leaders and coaches to be familiar with the latest research on effective professional development, such as the **PD Mechanisms | Why Coaching Works.**

4

PRACTICE & MORE PRACTICE

It's tempting to wait until coaches are fully trained before giving them opportunities to practise their coaching skills, but experience is critical in building their capacity. Actually working with teachers helps new coaches develop the case knowledge that makes them effective.

Use a *coach-and-be-coached* approach, where new coaches practise on each other first. This builds confidence and sharpens technique. Start with coaching prompts and scripts, then gradually remove them as competence grows. The key is to get them stuck in — practice is the best way to start.

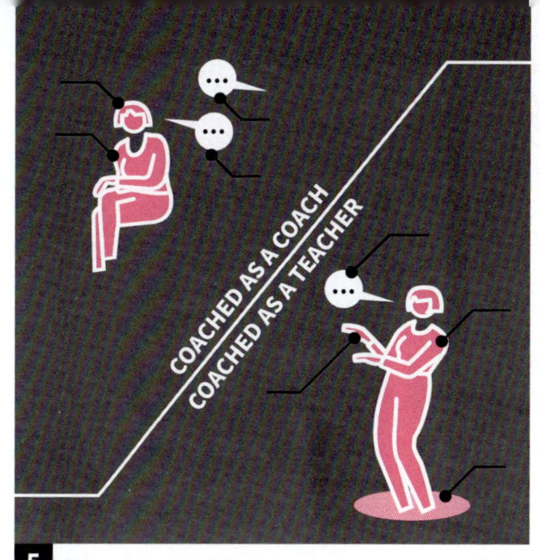

5

COACH ON COACHING & TEACHING

It's crucial that teachers selected as coaches are not exempt from being coached themselves. If coaches aren't coached, it can lead to resentment and hierarchy. Instead, coaches might receive double the coaching — first, by being coached as coaches. Visit lessons together, join their training sessions, watch their coaching conversations, then provide feedback. This adds rigour and ensures coaching quality. Second, coach them as teachers. While this can be time-consuming, it's worth it. Coaches need to be at the top of their game in the classroom, walking the walk, not just talking the talk.

WHAT?

The What? section includes nearly 50 ideas for coaches and leaders, organised across the six phases of our coaching process model. Each phase builds on the last, supporting a realistic and sustainable approach to developing teachers individually or in teams. We hope these ultra-practical guides serve as a useful manual for both new and experienced coaches, as well as middle and senior leaders working to implement a coaching approach in their schools or teams.

WALKTHRU **WHAT?** SERIES

CONDITIONS & CULTURE

01

It is essential that schools and colleges create an environment in which all teachers feel trusted and supported; an environment where coaching is taken seriously and is a normalised part of everyday practice. This series offers important guidance on building trust, promoting collaboration and involving everybody in the process. It includes practical steps to help leaders navigate accountability tensions and explores how team coaching and co-construction help embed a culture where professional development is shared, valued and celebrated.

BUILDING TRUST

Trust is built through clarity and consistency. Teachers are more likely to engage when expectations are visible, roles are understood and boundaries are respected. They also need to see that the process is valued across the school — not treated as optional, temporary or superficial.

This WalkThru sets out the core conditions that help coaching become established and taken seriously: a shared understanding of purpose, defined responsibilities, clear protocols and a commitment to seeing it through.

1

WHAT COACHING IS — AND ISN'T

Make it clear that coaching exists to improve teaching, not to evaluate it. It's not part of appraisal, capability or compliance. Say this explicitly and often — not just once in a launch session, but in every cycle and every meeting. Frame coaching as both a professional entitlement and responsibility.

It's not a bolt-on, an audit tool or a hoop to jump through. It's a focused space to think, rehearse and refine — because great teaching takes deliberate effort. Every message, every routine, every coaching move should reinforce that coaching is here to support improvement, not monitor it.

2

ROLES

Be clear from the start about who's responsible for what within the coaching process. Avoid parading coaches as expert teachers — this usually undermines trust. What matters most is that coaches have great knowledge and are genuinely interested in helping others improve.

- Who decides the teaching and learning focus?
- Who leads the training and coaching?
- Who visits who?

If coaches are also team leaders or line managers, acknowledge the overlap and navigate it carefully.

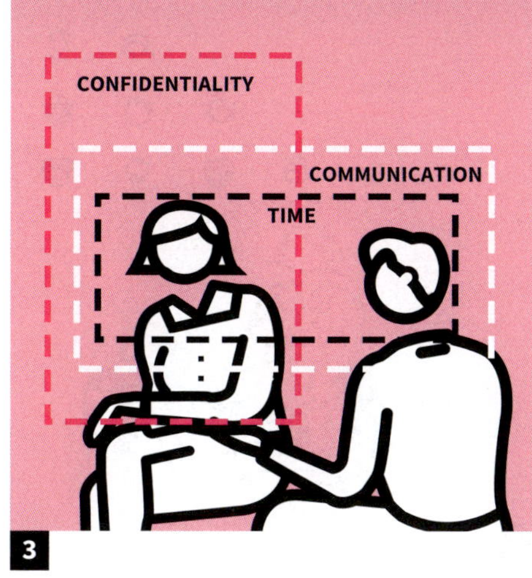

BOUNDARIES

Set and stick to clear boundaries around confidentiality, time and communication. Be upfront: what will be kept between coach and teacher, and what, if anything, might be shared more widely?

Never let coaching feel like a backchannel to senior leadership. If teachers think you're a spy for SLT, they'll disengage or shut down. This is especially important when using video — be precise about who sees it, who owns it and how it will be used.

4

EXPECTATIONS

Be clear about what each session involves and what teachers are expected to bring. Share your coaching materials with all staff so everyone knows what the process looks like. Model a typical coaching conversation in whole-staff training so it's demystified from the start.

Set expectations around timing, frequency, feedback formats and how the work will be recorded.

5

PERMANENCE

Coaching should feel like part of how the school works, not a passing gimmick. If it feels temporary, teachers are less likely to invest. Sustainable trust comes from follow-through. Log what's agreed. Follow up. Show that the work has teeth — that it matters, and that it's not going away. Publish a clear, long-term vision for coaching and professional learning so teachers understand where it's heading and how it fits with everything else.

Teachers need to know that their effort counts — and that coaching will still be there when things get busy.

COACHING SOME v. COACHING ALL

Setting up a universal system in a school requires a level of capacity that needs to be developed over time. Sometimes it's not realistic to involve every teacher in sustained one-to-one instructional coaching because the coaching capacity isn't yet sufficient.

However, there are dangers in creating subgroups within a staff body. Who is coached and who isn't? If coaching is important, why would anyone be left out? These questions need to be addressed.

1

ENGAGE EVERY TEACHER IN GROUP/ TEAM COACHING AS STANDARD

It's usually possible to ensure every teacher is involved in collective coaching cycles where action steps are agreed within teams or small groups.

With that in place for everyone, a cohort of teachers might also be coached one-to-one, dovetailing their individual and group agendas. This way everyone is involved in some form of coaching process; it's universal.

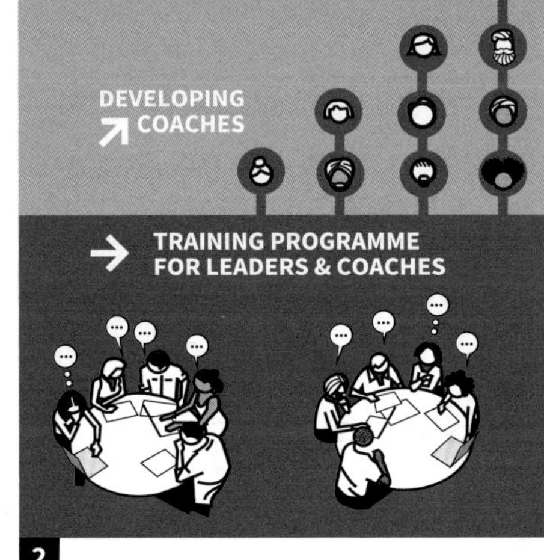

2

BUILD COACHING CAPACITY & COHORT SIZE IN PARALLEL

With a training programme in place for leaders and coaches to develop their skills, it's possible to be confident in the quality of the coaching taking place, gradually enabling more people to operate as coaches — either of individuals or pairs or small groups.

An alternative is to train everyone in school to be coaches simultaneously, coaching in pairs, but this requires a significant commitment to ensure the quality is adequate.

3

RUN PIONEER PILOT PROGRAMMES

When getting started with coaching, running a pilot programme is very powerful, supporting your school or college to learn how it can work in practice in your context.

Select a cohort of participants or volunteers willing to engage fully to test out the whole process over a period of months. Ideally, the pilot group includes a range of teachers so lessons can be learned that apply to everyone.

4

COACH ACROSS THE EXPERIENCE & EXPERTISE PROFILE

It can be problematic and even toxic in a school if coaching is associated with capability processes or teachers perceived as *weak*. It's vital to establish the principle that coaching can support every teacher at any career stage or level of expertise.

If you have a subgroup of teachers involved in one-to-one coaching, include experienced, expert teachers as well as new teachers or anyone that is struggling.

5

MAKE IT BUILT-IN, NOT OPT-IN

There are some principles to navigate around consent: coaching people individually against their will won't work and can be considered unethical.

However, if you want to support all children to succeed, and you believe professional learning is vital, it is also unwise to accept an opt-out culture.

The solution is to build it into the fabric of school life: everyone does coaching — either in teams, groups or individually.

CO-CONSTRUCTION | BUILD IT, DON'T SEND IT

In too many schools, feedback is still something that's sent or delivered — not built. Whether typed up, dropped into a form or spoken as judgement, it often bypasses the teacher entirely. That kind of feedback isn't just ineffective — it's disrespectful.

Co-constructed feedback is different. It involves teachers in the sense-making process, prompting them to think deeply about their classroom practice. It also makes meaningful action far more likely. This stance isn't just preferable — we'd argue that it's a core starting point for any effective PD system.

1 MAKE TALK EQUITABLE

Coaching dialogue should feel like a conversation between equals. Position yourself as a sounding board — you're not there to judge, and it shouldn't feel hierarchical. Show genuine interest in the teacher's perspective before offering your own. Affirm what they've noticed, then build on it with curiosity. If you have insights to share, offer them gently. Your contribution should support the teacher's thinking, not override it. In team sessions, use democratic structures like **Think, Pair, Share** or **Cold Calling** to create space for each person to speak before moving to shared sense-making.

2 CHOOSE YOUR WORDS CAREFULLY

Great coaching relies on calm, deliberate language that prompts reflection, not resistance. Keep your phrasing neutral, student-focused and purposeful. Avoid commentary that might come across as judgemental or imposing. Use the steps in **Cognitive Monitoring | Withholding Judgement** to help you reframe your ideas into useful prompts that help the teacher see more, using this as the basis for professional dialogue.

If you're running a team conversation, guide it without dominating. Think hand on the rudder, not at the helm.

3

TALK! DON'T SEND IT OR GIVE IT

Feedback is only meaningful when it's shared and understood in dialogue. Never rely on written feedback (e.g. email, lesson report) alone. It risks being misinterpreted or dismissed — and shows a lack of professional respect. Treat lesson visits as preparation for a real conversation, not a substitute.

Offer your insights in service of joint sense-making, not as an unwanted *gift of feedback*. If the teacher shares something you had noted, affirm it. If your view contrasts, share with humility and explore it together. You won't find that kind of nuance in an email!

4

USE QUESTIONS TO MEDIATE THINKING

Good questions reveal the teacher's thinking and help clarify their next moves. The teacher must do the heavy thinking — they're the one who has to act on it. Ask questions to **Build Clarity** and **Build Insight** to surface intentions, interpretations and perceptions. Prompts like 'What were you hoping to see?' or 'What did you notice about...?' anchor the conversation in specific moments and focus attention on student learning.

Avoid fishing for faults or steering the teacher towards your own conclusions — the goal is to support clearer thinking, not to correct.

5

DESIGN NEXT STEPS TOGETHER

Next steps should be co-created and context-specific, not dictated by the coach or decided in advance. Teachers are far more likely to resist or reject actions they haven't had a say in or don't see value in. Use **Questions to Build Action** to arrive at ideas that feel workable, relevant and worth testing. What matters is that any next step makes sense to the teacher and fits their classroom.

When working with teams, look for action steps that individuals can personalise while still contributing to the shared goal.

COGNITIVE MONITORING | WITHHOLDING JUDGEMENT

Sometimes, however well-intended, our language conveys unintentional meaning. Reframing feedback so that it is student-focused, not teacher-focused, and ensuring it is specific and actionable rather than ambiguous, can make our coaching more effective. This is a core part of coaching in the personal domain.

Teachers need to feel that the process is for them, not being done to them. That means avoiding language that feels judgemental or directive. The focus should always be on student impact, not the coach's opinion about how the lesson should have been taught.

1

REFRAMING

Feedback that focuses directly on the actions of the teacher can feel personal and judgemental. Instead, reframe your observations and insights so that they are student-focused. Feedback that focuses on the performance of students is much more likely to be received as formative by the teacher.

Instead of saying, 'You didn't explain photosynthesis very well,' say, 'Students seemed to struggle with the explanation of photosynthesis.'

Instead of 'You didn't give enough thinking time,' say, 'Some students might have benefitted from a little more time to think.'

2

AMBIGUITY & VAGUENESS

Teachers can't act on feedback that is nebulous or ambiguous. Telling a teacher 'That was a great lesson!' feels good but isn't necessarily helpful. What made the lesson great? Which specific features were effective, and why?

Instead, use precise, student-focused feedback:

'The class moved from independent work to paired work really fluently — they all knew who their talk-partners were.'

Make clear which specific elements of the teacher's practice are working well, by virtue of their impact on students.

3

THE PROBLEM WITH 'YOU'

Feedback can be problematic when it is aimed directly at the teacher. For example, 'When you explained the task, you didn't check that all of your students understood,' might as well be 'You should have, but you didn't.' The problem with 'you' is that it can come across as accusatory and judgemental. Of course, you can't avoid the word entirely, but you should be careful around how you're using it. Reframing as 'Some of the students were unsure about what they needed to do here — did you notice that?' shifts the focus from the actions of the teacher to the reaction of the students.

4

THE PROBLEM WITH 'I'

Guess what? Most teachers don't want to hear how an observer might have taught their lesson better than they did!

Feedback such as 'I might have chosen to live-model that activity' or 'I would have given them more time on that comprehension task' rarely lands well because it implies that 'I could have done it better.'

Keep your focus on the students — 'How well did the students get on with the comprehension task?' — and keep your own preferences at bay!

5

TACKLE SELF-CRITICISM

In feedback conversations, it's common for the teacher to want to home in on what they felt they did well or not so well. You should listen to their reflections of course, but don't indulge them.

Instead, keep nudging the focus back onto the students: 'That's an interesting reflection — what did that mean for the students?' or 'Okay — and what did you see that made you think that?'

RESOLVING ACCOUNTABILITY TENSIONS

In many schools and systems, teacher accountability is regarded as a key plank in efforts to raise standards. This usually involves leaders undertaking a few *formal observations* each year, leading to a detailed report with a list of issues the teacher should address. This can be accompanied by various other compliance checks and an evaluation of student outcomes.

While agreeing that teachers should be accountable for the quality of their work, some modes of quality assurance (QA) can be counterproductive, undermining the developmental approach we advocate. How do we find the balance?

1

FROM QUALITY ASSURANCE TO TEACHER DEVELOPMENT

The QA model tends to place unjustified weight on leaders' role as experts capable of judging teachers' quality, then issuing guidance or directives about what they should do differently. However, this model is fundamentally flawed, ignoring the evidence about how teachers actually improve. Even expert observers may not accurately evaluate quality of teaching and even then they cannot merely direct a teacher's actions remotely.

An emphasis on teacher development places teachers' learning at the centre and requires a rethink on the nature of QA.

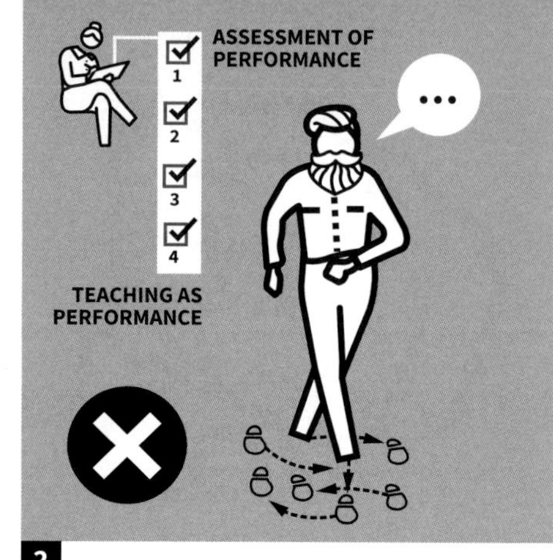

2

FROM FORMAL LESSON OBSERVATIONS TO LEARNING WALKS

Formal lesson observations, typically conducted by leaders 2-3 times per year, place disproportionate emphasis on delivering set-piece lessons that meet the school's criteria for a positive judgement. These lessons become performative rather than revealing typical issues the teacher experiences.

Learning walks are much better! Here, leaders drop into multiple lessons for, say, 10 minutes each, engaging with the lesson and the learning. They are low stakes, quick and can be repeated many times across the year capturing typicality.

3

FROM OBSERVER REPORTS TO TEACHER RECORDS

Reports on one lesson serve virtually no developmental purpose, especially if written without any discussion with the teacher. We advocate giving teachers ownership, using records to track progress with actions across the coaching cycle. Make them:

LEAN | only record key issues and actions; quick to complete in minutues.

SHARED | co-owned by teacher and coach to track progress in a visible manner.

ACTION-FOCUSED | record agreed action steps not detailed reviews of previous lessons.

4

FROM INTENTIONS TO ACCOUNTABLE ACTIONS

In truth, there should be greater and deeper accountability embedded in a sustained coaching process because of the regular follow-up on agreed action steps. Whether coaching individuals or a team, each teacher declares their intentions based on the feedback conversation. However, this is not merely a vague hope for future actions — it needs to be sincere commitment to real change. Part of a healthy productive coaching process is that we check to see whether a teacher is following through on their commitments. Here is where accountability truly lies: doing what we say we'll do.

5

FROM SHORT-TERM COMPLIANCE TO SUSTAINED CHANGE

A further benefit of a strong coaching culture is that we focus on shifting habits over time. We are not interested in *speed camera* behaviours where teachers might follow agreed protocols or perform a WalkThru routine when being observed, but not the rest of the time. Where schools use routine learning walks, capturing typicality, and then undertake structured feedback conversations using **The 5Ps Framework**, short-term compliance ceases to be an issue. The culture is more sincere — we aim for sustained change, and teachers' motivation towards achieving their goals is much greater.

THREE-POINT COMMUNICATION

As Stone and Heen (2014) point out, feedback is often problematic. However well-intentioned and skilful the coach, the teacher receiving the feedback still feels vulnerable. But none of this is the fault of either party. It's more to do with the structure of the situation. When the dialogue is positive, speaking face-to-face is the best and most natural dynamic. However, when the agenda is serious — maybe even difficult — attempting to increase the personal tone within this arrangement is often counterproductive. There is a solution.

1

NOTICE HOW TWO-POINT FEEDBACK IS FRAUGHT

Through our cultural upbringing, and even training, we become convinced that face-to-face communication is the best method for every circumstance. It feels so natural and authentic. And, as teachers, we are very good and practised at it.

But such a dynamic increases the emotions of both parties, whether they're positive or negative. So, given the sensibilities of the feedback process, it might be time to master **Three-Point Communication** to avoid the negative results of difficult conversations but not to evade their purpose.

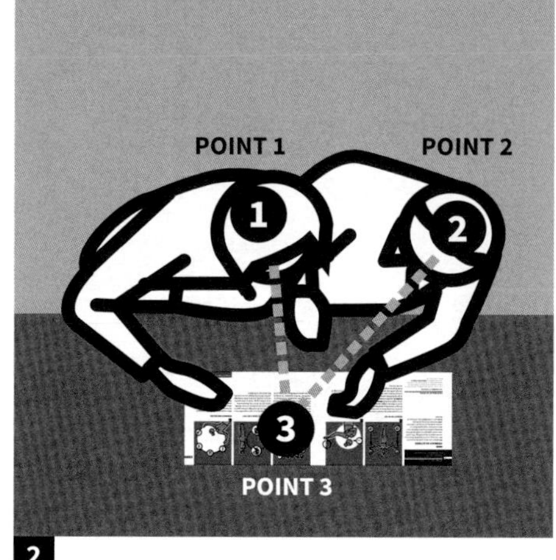

2

TRY LEARNING SIDE BY SIDE

Side-by-side learning can be a physical reality in addition to being only a metaphor. By adding a third point — here a WalkThru — both parties share the same perspective. A detachment gap now exists between the coach and her feedback. Emotions subside; an objective focus pervades.

When the content is volatile, the communicator wants to display the information visually — the third point.

3

FINE-TUNE TWO ASPECTS

If possible, try sitting at the corner of a table. This makes it more natural, on occasion, to turn to your partner and briefly look at them, before returning to the third point.

The coach also uses her outer hand to point to an aspect of the WalkThru being discussed. By doing so, she doesn't obscure the teacher's view, nor closes off her body to the teacher. Pointing to what she is referring to in the visual helps the teacher avoid a cognitive lag as he searches to match words with the specific part of the image.

These two refinements are not essential but are nonetheless worth noting — even trying out.

4

CREATE PSYCHOLOGICAL SAFETY

Sitting side by side affords immediate benefits. The energy shifts from the relationship to the shared pursuit of the coaching conversation. Throughout, the focus remains *out there*, and references are made to the teacher in the image, not the one being coached.

NANCY DUARTE

A presentation that creates common ground has the potential to unite a diverse group of people toward a common purpose.

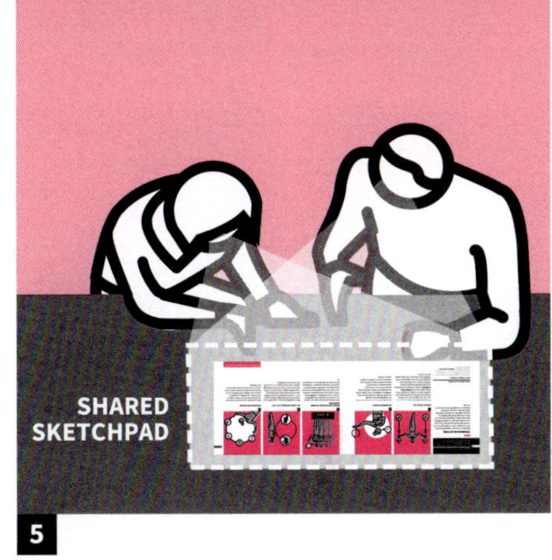

5

BUILD A PROBLEM-SOLVING PARTNERSHIP

By sustaining the conversation about the shared sketchpad, a strong sense of partnership is established. The sketchpad is usually applied to a personal psychology but in this instance its shared occupancy builds a feeling of joint problem-solving.

ERIC LUNZER

Everyone is looking down and checking what it says. Interactions are therefore object-centred and not person-centred.

TEAM COACHING; TEAM CULTURE

Our experience in the field suggests team coaching has a vital role across the system. It's a mistake to insist *coaching* equates to the one-to-one scenario.

Teams are the default home of teacher discussion, and where we see effective teaching across a school, there are always effective teams driving curriculum thinking and collective action. One-to-one coaching can support this but is never sufficient on its own. Team coaching can drive rapid change serving as a platform for all other professional learning.

1

HARNESS THE POWER OF COLLECTIVE ACTION

Working collectively and collaboratively can be highly motivating, with teachers sharing the many common challenges they experience and exchanging common solutions.

That sense of *we're all in this together* can be a powerful driver of change. Teachers can have individual professional goals and needs while also being strongly aligned to a team agenda.

2

SET UP TEAM COACHING CYCLES

It's a simple pragmatic option to repurpose team meetings that already exist in a school calendar to serve as coaching sessions. These can then be linked up to form cycles:

MEETING 1 | Establish team goals around a common problem.

MEETING 2 | Review feedback from observations, refining action steps.

MEETING 3 | Review feedback from learning walks and agree next steps.

3

ESTABLISH THE COACHING PROTOCOL FOR EACH SESSION

The same protocol for individual coaching can be applied to teams. **Team Conversations** applies the Bambrick-Santoyo 5Ps protocol to team sessions and it works brilliantly.

Once established, the Precise Praise and Probe steps allow colleagues to reaffirm progress with enacting techniques and to explore persistent problems — always with a sense of solidarity and mutual support.

4

LINK OBSERVATION TO TEAM MEETING CYCLES

With this approach it's important that coaching sessions are informed by the reality check that observations provide. This could be:

- Learning walks by the leader.
- Paired observations with everyone observing a colleague live or via a video.
- Planned individual observations by a coach or team leader.

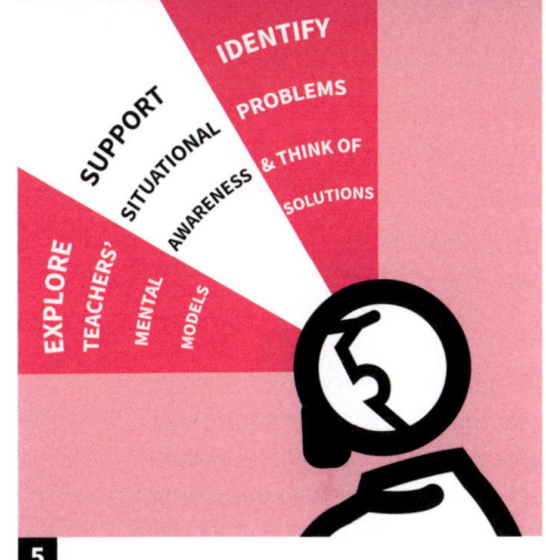

5

TRAIN TEAM LEADERS TO APPLY THE 5PS APPROACH

Making the switch from regular team meeting protocols to running them like a coaching session requires some training.

Leaders need to adapt the mindset of a coach — seeking to explore each teacher's mental models, supporting them to develop their situation awareness, identifying problems and thinking of solutions.

Structured planning tools using the 5Ps for meetings are available on our website.

A CULTURE OF COLLABORATION

We see the greatest impact in schools that take care to build a culture of collaboration. This means a whole-school commitment to improving teaching and learning. It starts with a shared belief: the work matters, and it belongs to everyone. No one is the finished article. Teaching is a complex craft, and as Dylan Wiliam reminds us, one lifetime isn't enough to master it.

In these schools, everyone is invested. Success is noticed and celebrated — not occasionally, but as part of the culture.

Co-written with Nikki Sullivan.

1

BUILD A SHARED SENSE OF THE *WHY*

Make sure everyone understands what coaching is for and why it matters. Use consistent messages to connect coaching with what matters most: improving teaching so that students learn more. Be explicit about the purpose behind your school's professional learning approach — over-communicate this in staff briefings, team meetings and coaching conversations. The message should be explicit: coaching isn't about performance management. It's about helping teachers get better, because students deserve the best version of us.

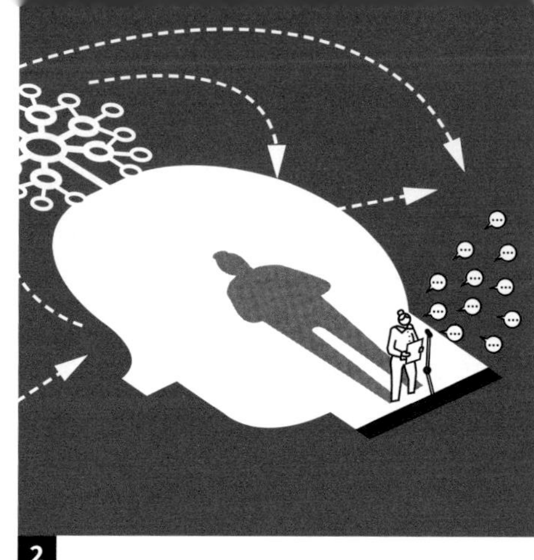

2

BUILD A COMMON LANGUAGE

Teachers can't collaborate on improving practice unless they're speaking the same language. An important starting point is a shared understanding of how learning happens (i.e. **The Learning Model**) so that learning problems can be surfaced and discussed. Next, build a common language around teaching and learning. The **WalkThrus toolkit** can provide the basis for this, supported by frameworks like **Rosenshine's Principles of Instruction**. Do the same for your coaching system — be transparent about what's involved and how you'll talk about it, so there are no surprises.

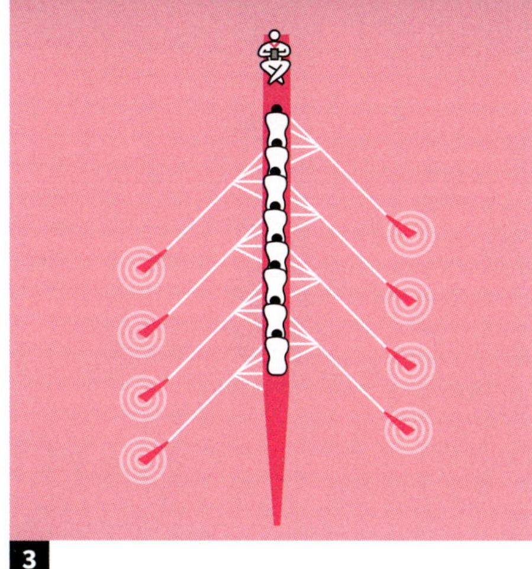

3

BUILD BUY-IN

Things start to move when everyone rows together — an alignment of **Three-Stream CPD** with leaders and teachers pulling in the same direction. It's important at every level to agree what matters most and commit to making it happen. Teams need clarity on how their coaching connects to school priorities. Individual teachers should know how their goals contribute to something bigger. Make it clear that coaching isn't an extra — it's embedded. When everyone sees the purpose, the plan and their part in it, coaching becomes a collective effort that keeps students at the centre.

4

BUILD PROFESSIONAL CHALLENGE

A low-stakes, open-door culture, where colleagues and leaders drop in on each other to build insights and share their practice as part of daily life, is a central part of collective improvement. Teachers become more open to discussing their classes because the culture is low threat, high challenge — that's the key. Nobody is the finished product. Everyone can make small changes that shift things for students — and we want everyone up for this challenge. Coaching should feel like a professional challenge teachers want to meet, not pressure they'd rather avoid.

5

BUILD SHARED SUCCESS

When teachers see that their work is noticed, valued and making a difference, motivation builds. Share the wins — big or small — across teams and staff meetings. Let teachers talk about what they've tried and how it helped.

Make it normal for staff to say, 'Here's what I've been working on.' This reinforces a culture of continuous learning — where coaching belongs to everyone, not just a few.

DIAGNOSE & DESIGN

Effective coaching starts with a clear diagnosis. The Diagnose & Design section helps coaches identify real classroom challenges by observing where students are struggling. It offers practical tools for using lesson visits, data and video to build insight, test hunches and explore learning problems. Drawing on research into how learning happens and why it sometimes fails, this section supports coaches to think clearly, spot patterns and design purposeful goals that connect teacher actions to student learning.

SOLVING LEARNING PROBLEMS

At the heart of effective coaching is a Problem-Solution dynamic. Classrooms are complex, and coaching helps teachers make sense of that complexity by surfacing learning problems and acting on solutions. The goal is to find out why students struggle, working alongside the teacher to uncover root causes and avoid jumping to conclusions based on assumptions.

Then, select WalkThrus techniques that can help address the problems, and help teachers to embed them.

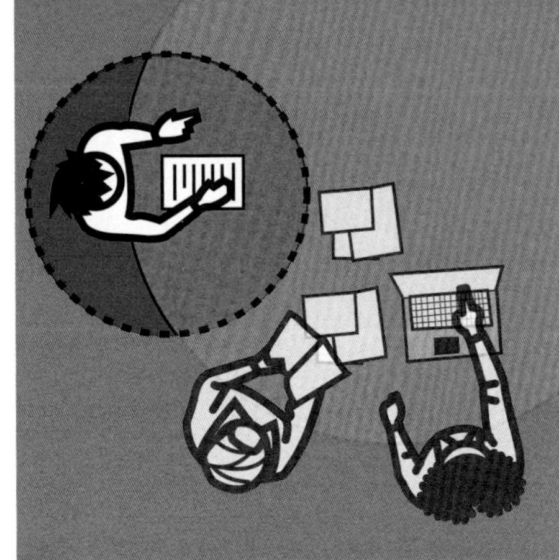

1

LOOK AT STUDENT PERFORMANCE

First, try to identify where students are succeeding and where they seem to be finding learning difficult. Look out for symptoms of **Common Problems** — these are often a good starting point and it can often be more productive than trying to look at everything at once.

Combine lesson study with supporting data, such as formative assessments and student work. Use the steps in **Using Data** for guidance.

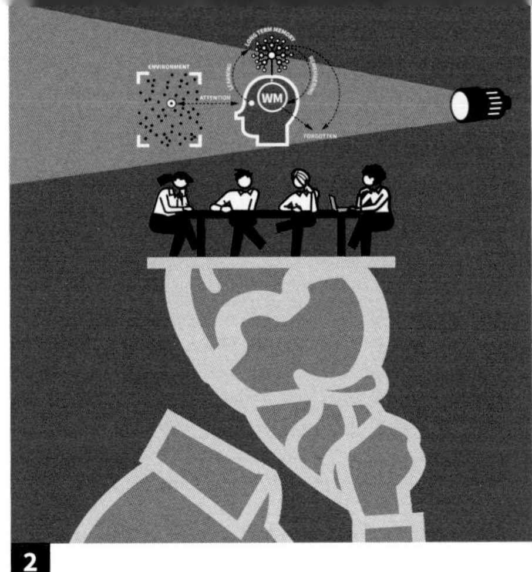

2

SENSE-MAKE

Work with the teacher to make sense of what has been observed in lessons, alongside any useful data that has been collected.

What does it suggest? Use **The Learning Model** to guide the focus towards root causes, rather than assumptions. Make this a co-constructed dialogue — the teacher and the coach both sharing insights — where the goal is to use the data to paint a clear picture of student performance. Use **Questions to Build Clarity** and **Questions to Build Insight** to surface and examine important ideas.

3

IDENTIFY WHERE STUDENTS ARE STRUGGLING OR COULD IMPROVE

Once you've built a shared understanding of the problem you're trying to solve, identify the precise points where students are struggling or could improve.

This might be a desired change in behaviour, thinking, participation or confidence of material being studied. What would the teacher like to see the students doing, saying, thinking or achieving differently next time?

The more precise you can be, the more accurate the selection of strategies can be.

4

EXPLORE STRATEGIES TO SUPPORT THE CHANGE

Use the menu of options from the WalkThrus playbook to identify specific techniques to help support the change. Begin by exploring a cluster of multiple-potential solutions — in detail so that you can make good decisions about their usefulness — then focus in on a single technique.

The WalkThrus **Problem-Solution Tool** has been designed for this purpose — to help you zoom in from big problems to individual starting points.

5

DESIGN A GOAL

We discuss the importance of goal setting frequently in this book. Without a clear goal, coaching conversations rarely lead to action.

Follow the steps in **Goal Setting: If… Then… So That…** to design a goal that represents the desired change, the action to be taken and the success criteria. Then, help the teacher to meet the goal by applying **The WalkThrus Coaching Process**.

COMMON PROBLEMS [1]

Teachers face common challenges in the classroom. While each school, subject and lesson is different, certain difficulties appear again and again; they are universal because they are the unavoidable implications of our cognitive architecture.

The next two WalkThrus explore 10 common problems, ranging from securing attention to guiding effective retrieval practice. As a coach, you'll encounter these issues in nearly every lesson you observe. The key is recognising them and knowing how to respond in a way that best supports the teachers you are working with.

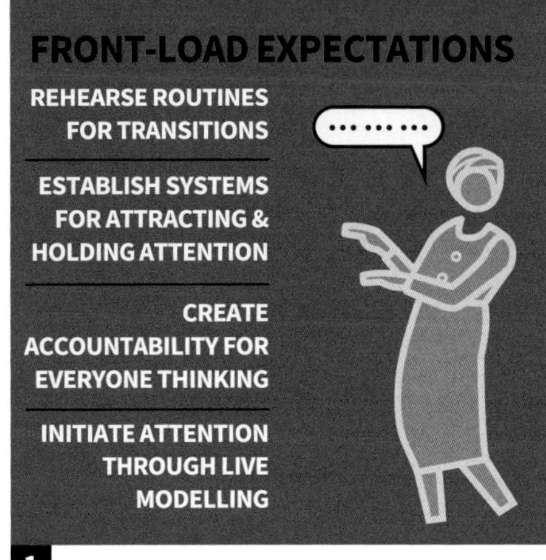

1

SECURING ATTENTION

If students aren't paying attention, they aren't learning. A core challenge for teachers is to secure the attention of all students in the class. This is a prerequisite for any learning to follow and yet it is difficult. Be ready to spot and support teachers to solve this problem using techniques to secure and hold attention at a whole-class level. For example, use **Signal, Pause, Insist** to design a routine for attention, and keep students cognitively engaged by using high-ratio routines like **Live Modelling, Cold Call** and **Think, Pair, Share**.

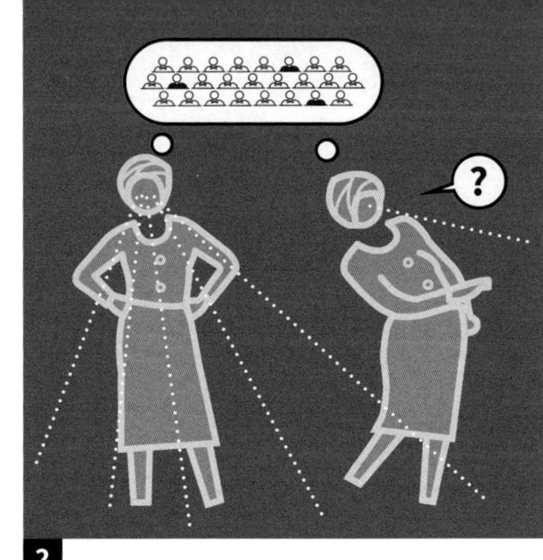

2

INCLUSIVE QUESTIONING

It's common to see classrooms that rely on a handful of students to carry the discussion while others switch off. It's common for some students to be disconnected from questioning processes and teachers often find it hard to involve the least confident or the least engaged students. Help teachers build questioning routines that involve everyone in deep thinking. **Cold Call, Think, Pair, Share** and **Show-Me Boards** make participation the norm, not the exception. Help teachers to spot the students who routinely opt out and adjust their questioning so every student is involved and thinking.

3

PROMPTING DEEP THINKING

We want all students thinking deeply about their learning, but this doesn't always happen on its own. Thinking hard is effortful — we tend to favour quick intuition over deep thinking — and creating the conditions that get all students thinking hard about the right thing is a real challenge. Help teachers to build academic rigour with **Pitch It Up** and use **Silence Is Golden** to create conditions that allow full concentration without disruption. Deeper questioning techniques, like **Process Questions, Probing Questions** and **Say It Again Better**, can also prompt students into deeper thinking.

4

SECURING PUPIL TALK

Well-organised classroom talk ensures every pupil has the opportunity to rehearse ideas, practise explanations and engage in productive discussion using key vocabulary. But, talk routines must include individual accountability — no pupil should be able to sit back while others do the thinking. Work with the teacher to establish a strong **Think, Pair, Share** routine that engages the whole class in structured talk. Use **Deliberate Vocabulary Development** to build oral fluency, and make **Class Discussion** a regular feature of lessons.

5

LANDING EXPLANATIONS

Explanation is one of the most powerful tools at a teacher's disposal. But the challenge is providing students with an explanation that they can not only make sense of, but that also provides a conceptual framework that consolidates their understanding of an idea. Support the teacher to plan their explanations deliberately using **Giving an Explanation**. Help them to refine their explanations using **Dual Coding, Analogies** and **Examples & Non-Examples**.

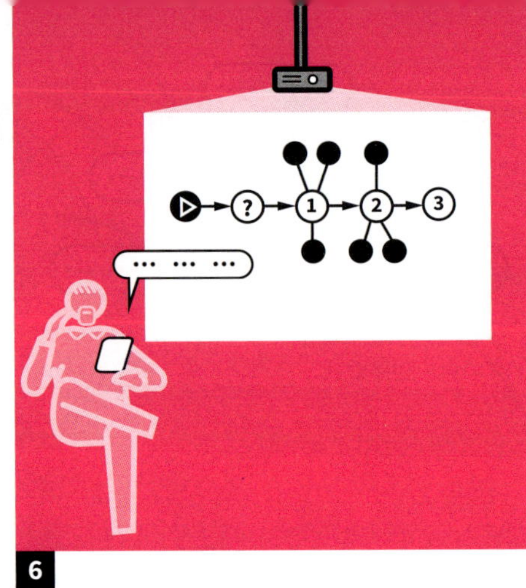

6

PROVIDING MODELS

Modelling is central to effective teaching, but balancing modelling time with checking for understanding is a constant challenge. Some students grasp concepts quickly, while others might struggle to apply what they've seen. Support teachers to enact an effective **Modelling Handover**, using **Live Modelling** and **Worked Examples & Backward Fading** to guide students towards independence. Help them to build a repertoire of **Checking for Understanding** so that they can reliably check what students have understood.

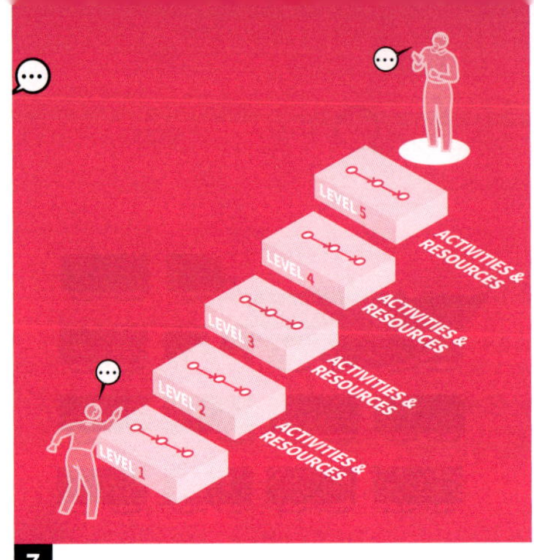

7

LADDER OF DIFFICULTY

Help teachers structure challenge so students keep progressing. Try to spot students who are ready to apply knowledge and those who are still consolidating. A well-planned **Ladder of Difficulty** ensures incremental steps, building fluency before application. Help the teacher to **Pitch It Up** to raise expectations, **Teach to the Top** to maintain challenge with support, and **Scaffolding** to help all students to succeed. The goal is to manage challenge, not avoid it — ensuring students keep climbing rather than getting stuck.

8

CHECK FOR UNDERSTANDING

Learning is invisible — without real feedback, there's no way to know what's been learned or where students have struggled. Help teachers establish frequent and reliable **Strategies to Check for Understanding** such as **Cold Call, Think, Pair, Share** and **Show-Me Boards**. Watch for poor proxies for understanding such as thumbs-up/thumbs-down. Checking should inform next steps by identifying gaps, addressing misconceptions or moving forward while also reinforcing learning as students retrieve and consolidate ideas.

9

GUIDING EFFECTIVE RETRIEVAL

Retrieval practice only works when teachers run it with purpose. Students can only retrieve what has been previously learned, so retrieval must reinforce key knowledge and connect to what comes next. Support teachers in using **Quizzing** to check understanding efficiently, **Weekly & Monthly Review** to consolidate learning over time and **A Repertoire of Retrieval Routines** to ensure varied, effective checks. Retrieval should be a diagnostic tool, guiding decisions on what to reteach and revisit rather than assuming high success rates mean learning is secure.

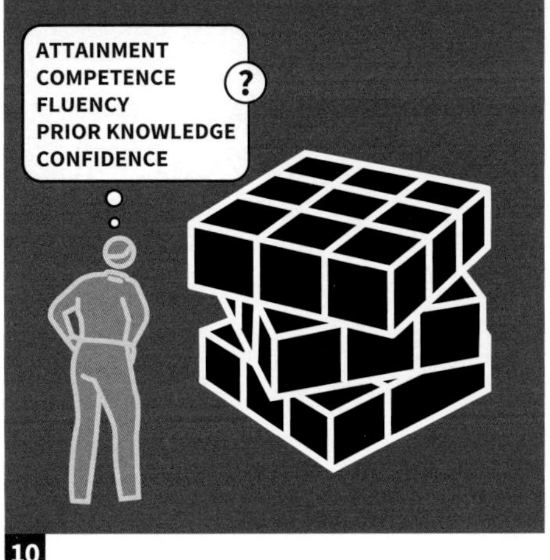

10

MIXED-ATTAINING CLASSES

Every class includes a mix of attainment, confidence and prior knowledge. Fixed labels of *ability* can be misleading — the real challenge is managing this variation effectively. Support teachers in using **SEND: Aim High, Plan Support** to maintain and guide high expectations for all students. Use **Thresholds & Pathways** to support and guide student progress at different rates, and **Responsive Lesson Planning** to adapt the curriculum in real time. The goal is to keep learning accessible without lowering challenge or relying on rigid differentiation.

COMMON PROBLEMS [2]

When tackling these common learning problems, remember that no single technique is likely to provide a complete solution. As a coach, work with teachers to diagnose the issue, analyse and understand its causes, and zoom in to a range of potential strategies. The Problem-Solution Cluster Tool, available online to WalkThrus members, offers a structured approach to this process, mapping common challenges to multiple solutions.

LESSON VISITS & LEARNING WALKS

Visiting lessons to see teachers and students at work is a core part of a coach's role. But it's often done poorly — too vague, too high-stakes or too disconnected from the teacher's goals and student learning. The purpose of a coaching visit is simple: to help the teacher make better sense of what's happening in their classroom and how they can create better conditions for learning.

Coaching visits are there to help teachers get it right for their students — not to evaluate or judge. Keeping that purpose clear helps build trust.

1

ESTABLISH A CLEAR PURPOSE

Be explicit about why you're visiting the lesson, and always frame your focus through the lens of student learning. For example: 'I'm dropping in to see how the students are getting on with **Think, Pair, Share**' or 'I want to get a sense of how they're responding to your live modelling approach.'

When the reason for your presence is vague — or worse, feels evaluative — the visit quickly becomes a performance. Clarify the purpose beforehand and stick to it. Moving the goalposts mid-visit undermines the process.

2

SELECT A FLOODLIGHT...

At the start of a new coaching cycle — when the aim is to diagnose a learning problem — or when the visit is part of a team cycle designed to spot common threads across classrooms, use a floodlight lens.
A floodlight lets you see patterns and shapes without zooming in on specific details.
For example:

- The extent to which all students are focusing their attention in lessons.
- How systematically the teacher checks for understanding.

The key here is that you're looking for a common or important problem to solve. Once you see it, you can zoom in.

3

...OR SPOTLIGHT

Use a spotlight lens to illuminate specific details — specific steps in a technique, or a key moment in the lesson, e.g. how productively students use their thinking time in a **Cold Call** routine, or the precision of a **Show-Me Board** reveal.

This works well when the focus has already been agreed. A tightly focused frame allows you to zoom in, unpick what's happening and share insights on what worked and why. It's especially effective for one-to-one coaching, or when a teacher is refining a specific technique and wants to improve the detail.

4

LOOK FOR LEARNING

Don't just focus on whether the teacher is performing the steps of a technique — look at what students are actually learning. It's possible to run **Think, Pair, Share** perfectly, but for student conversations to be superficial.

A teacher might follow the steps in **Live Modelling** with absolute fidelity, but students still aren't following. The steps matter — especially when a technique is new — but they aren't the whole picture. Look closely at what students are doing and saying. That's what tells you whether the technique is landing.

5

APPLY FILTERS

You're not there to judge the teacher's overall quality — you're there to help them make sense of their classroom and improve learning. Stay conscious of your biases and blind spots. We often give too much weight to our first impressions, last impressions or what we expected to see — all of which can throw you off course.

It's natural to form judgements, but it's rarely helpful. Apply a cognitive filter: suspend conclusions, hold impressions lightly and stay curious. Teaching is complex; we only ever see a snapshot of what's really happening in a classroom.

USING VIDEO

Video is one of the most powerful tools in coaching — it slows down the classroom, captures what's often missed and creates shared reference points for effective conversations. As Jim Knight puts it, it's rocket fuel for learning. But only when it's used carefully. For many teachers, recording themselves feels exposing — which means trust and transparency are essential.

This WalkThru will help you make video a practical, low-stakes part of your coaching.

1

AGREE PROTOCOLS & PURPOSE

Using video for coaching diagnosis is powerful, but it relies on trust. For many teachers, filming themselves feels daunting — they worry about how they look, how they sound and who might see it. This response is common and valid.

Make the process transparent and safe. The teacher controls what's recorded, when and who sees it. They retain full ownership — it's for them and their coach only. The aim isn't to fix a single moment, but to use it as a way into the day-to-day classroom experience of students. Don't force it. Build confidence and normalise video use over time.

2

OPT FOR A LOW-TECH APPROACH

It's easy to get carried away with video — multiple cameras, clip-on mics, tripods — but these often distract more than help. A low-tech approach is usually best. Subtle, unfussy recordings feel more authentic and cause less disruption.

Teacher and student behaviour shifts when filming feels like an event — keep it simple. Use a school iPad or Chromebook, ideally positioned in the front corner, over the teacher's shoulder, capturing as many students as possible. Don't edit or re-record because of minor interruptions — it's a snapshot of real life, and just a starting point.

3

FOCUS ON LEARNING

When reviewing the video, apply the same lens as you would in a live lesson. The goal is to understand what students are learning — not just whether the teacher is performing the steps of a technique. A teacher might run a textbook **Cold Call** routine, but some students might not be formulating a response. Or they might follow the steps for **Worked Examples** perfectly, but some students still aren't clear on how to emulate it independently. The technique matters, especially when it's new — but what matters more is what students know, do and understand as a result.

4

REWATCH INDEPENDENTLY

It sounds obvious, but lots of teachers avoid watching their video back — usually because it feels uncomfortable. But that reluctance can get in the way of the real benefits. Coaching is a shared process of noticing and sense-making — and that only works when both teacher and coach have watched the footage in advance. Video is just one source of information, not the full picture.

Its value comes when both teacher and coach come ready to compare notes, unpick what's working and build useful questions to move things forward.

5

ZOOM IN & OUT

The real benefit of video is that it can be paused and replayed. In live observations, moments come and go quickly — they're easy to miss, misread or interpret differently. Video gives you the chance to stop, rewind and look again. You can zoom in to specific details — the phrasing of a question, or a specific student's response — and take a much closer look. These details tell you whether the technique is actually working. Zooming in sharpens your focus; zooming out gives you perspective. Both matter.

USING DATA

Data should support improvement, not evaluate performance. In coaching, *data* means concrete, observable information about what students are doing, saying, writing and learning. It'll often be qualitative or impressionistic — what matters is that it helps the teacher reflect and make better decisions.

No single source tells the whole story, so use a range: observation, video, student work, curriculum materials and teacher reflections. Agree in advance what to focus on, then stick to it. A quick scan of whiteboards, a tally of disengaged students or a few underdeveloped answers in a discussion all count.

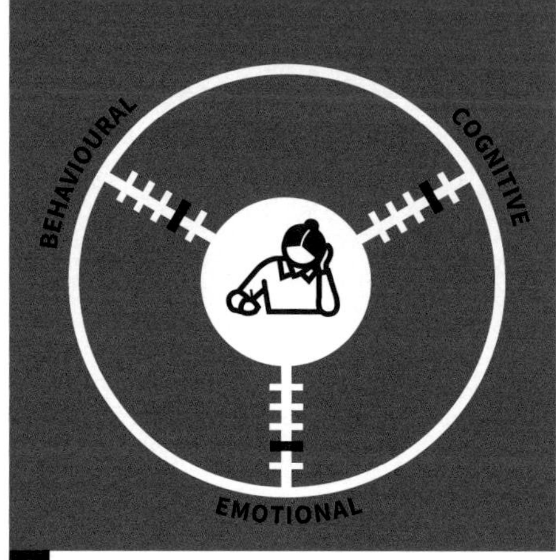

1

USE STUDENT ENGAGEMENT DATA

Collect engagement data (Knight, 2018) to get a sense of how well students are engaged with learning. There are three elements to consider:

BEHAVIOURAL | Which students are involved, on-task and following expectations?

COGNITIVE | Which students are thinking hard about the right thing, for the right reasons?

EMOTIONAL | Which students are confident and positive about their learning?

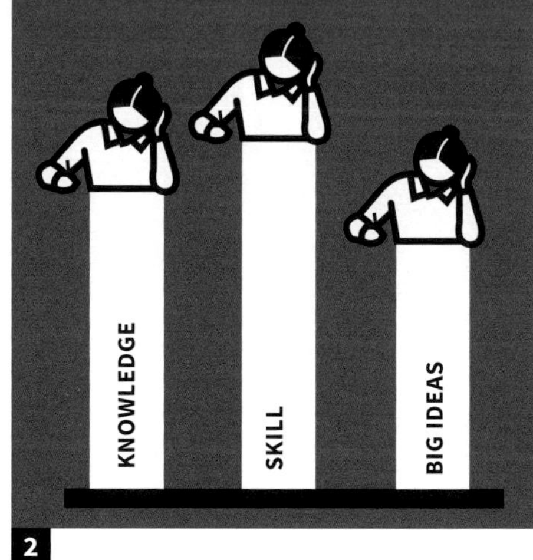

2

USE STUDENT LEARNING DATA

Learning data reveals how well students are learning in the moment. This comes from what you and the teacher notice during the lesson — what are students saying, doing and achieving? For example:

- A scan of **Show-Me Boards** reveals repeated errors that the teacher didn't catch while circulating.
- **Cold Calling** prompts clearer, more confident responses from students who usually stay quiet.

Use this kind of detail to support focused reflection and help the teacher make purposeful adjustments.

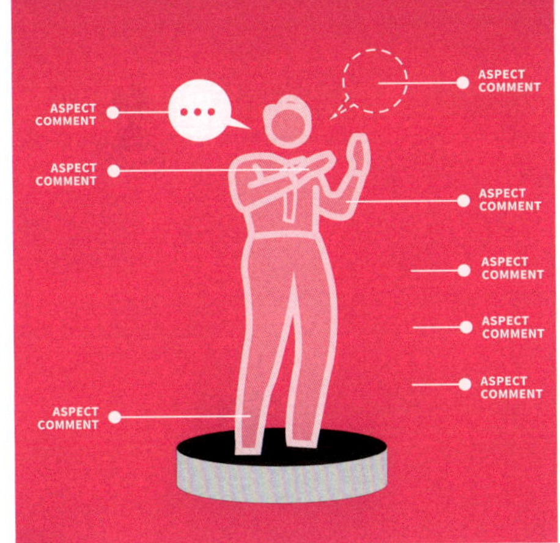

3

COLLECT TEACHING DATA

It's just as important for coaches to gather data on what teachers do: their in-the-moment decisions; how they apply techniques; and how they run the room.

Get stuck into the detail, such as: how many questions are asked, which students are selected and how many students are involved in follow-up questions; or the amount of thinking time given in **Think, Pair, Share**; or how long the teacher spends live modelling a maths problem on the board. Collecting teaching data provides insights that support more intentional teaching.

4

USE TO GET A CLEAR PICTURE OF REALITY

It is simply unrealistic to think that coaches or leaders could drop into a classroom and make an accurate diagnosis based on instinct alone.

Good data keeps us focused on learning — it makes the invisible visible. The key is to triangulate multiple data points to build an objective understanding of what is happening in the classroom.

5

USE TO INFORM GOAL SETTING

There's strong evidence behind the importance of goal setting in effective PD. But goals can only be effective if they are informed by good data.

Once you've built a clear picture of what's really happening in the classroom, use that insight to design effective goals. Use data to keep the goal rooted in reality.

Frame goals using the guidance in **Goal Setting: If… Then… So That…**.

HUNCHES & HYPOTHESES

Lessons are complex; it's often difficult to predict the effects of teachers' actions or the causes of their problems. It's important to work with this challenge rather than ignore it. Coaches can do this by recognising their hunches, turning them into hypotheses and testing them against evidence related to student learning.

Holding hypotheses lightly respects the uncertainty of teaching and creates space to figure out the causes.

SARAH COTTINGHATT

ADAM KOHLBECK

1

KNOW YOUR ROLE

Begin by understanding the coach's role when they observe lessons. Coaches have a broader but shallower mental model of the lesson: they see more but often understand less because the teacher knows more about the context and sometimes, the subject too. Use this broader view to spot something that might be limiting student learning. Be prepared to be wrong in your interpretation of the situation until checking the teacher's viewpoint.

Keep in mind that it's not the coach's role to be right or to have the perfect solution.

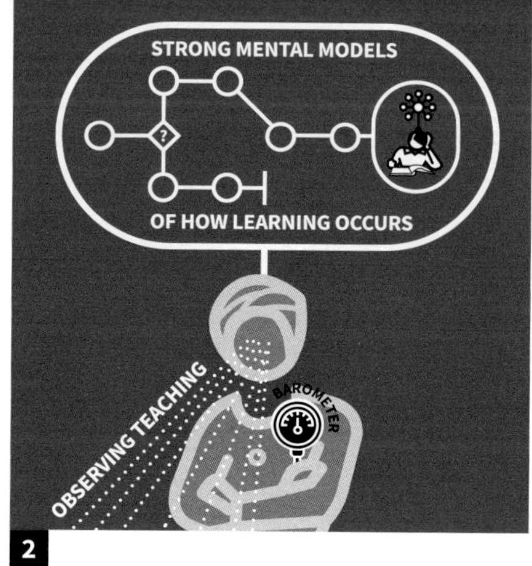

2

KNOW YOUR STUFF

When observing teaching, use strong mental models of how learning occurs and how great teaching can catalyse learning. These mental models become a barometer for whether actions are likely to support learning and a scaffold for identifying what matters most.

Avoid diagnosing the problem based on personal preferences as this decouples teaching from learning. This means it is unlikely to have the greatest impact and may erode trust with the teacher.

3

GET TRIPPED UP

Let strong mental models *catch* on weak moments. This will feel like getting tripped up because it's a sudden alertness to a situation.

Begin recording what's happening. Capture events non-judgementally — think stenographer not judge or jury. Prioritise situations that are upstream when it comes to learning: problems with attention will usually trump those around assessment. Form a hunch that there might be a problem worth coaching on but hold it very lightly — it may not be clear that it is impacting student learning just yet.

4

TEST YOUR HYPOTHESIS

Turn the hunch into a hypothesis — e.g. 'That explanation seemed to contain some very challenging vocabulary for these students' (hunch based on instinct) becomes 'That explanation seemed to contain some very challenging vocabulary for these students — they may struggle with the next task.'

Test the hypothesis against appropriate evidence by recording events, and checking the quality of students' work and their responses to questions. Tentatively conclude whether there is a learning problem at play but continue to hold it lightly — the teacher's viewpoint may also be necessary.

5

SHARE THE PROCESS

During the coaching conversation, be open about the process of forming a hunch and testing the hypothesis. Zoom in on the situation and ask the teacher to share what they noticed. Use the teacher's mental model to interpret the situation more clearly or sharpen their awareness. When the teacher's mental model needs developing, use tentative language to share what was noticed, remaining clear and concise.

For example: 'A lot of challenging vocabulary came up. That raised a question of whether students could understand. What evidence do we have about that afterwards?'

GOAL SETTING | IF... THEN... SO THAT...

When teachers define clear goals linked to their practice, they are more likely to act and improve.

The research is clear on the power of goal setting in PD — but too often, it's not applied in practice. Our fieldwork shows just how important this mechanism is — not just for individuals, but for teams.

The **If... Then... So That...** framework works because it underpins the Problem-Solution dynamic of great coaching: naming the problem, specifying the technique that might help and building clarity around what the intended change will look like.

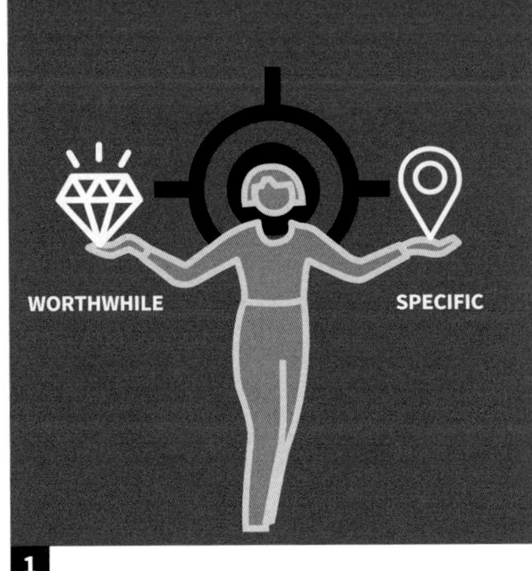

1

TWO KEY PRINCIPLES

There's plenty of guidance on setting goals — but in our experience, two principles matter most.

WORTHWHILE | It matters less who suggests the goal, and more that teachers accept it as important. Goals should solve real classroom problems — without personal relevance, not much will happen. This is especially challenging in team coaching, where shared goals are in play.

SPECIFIC | Link goals to specific actions. The more concrete they are — focused on real classroom scenarios — the more likely they are to be implemented.

2

IF...

Start with the problem: what needs to be different in the classroom? This is about identifying what the teacher wants to improve or see more of:

- If I want all students thinking hard about a question…
- If I want all students practising their explanations…

Be as precise as possible. The *If* should reflect a clear diagnosis and define a manageable, specific change.

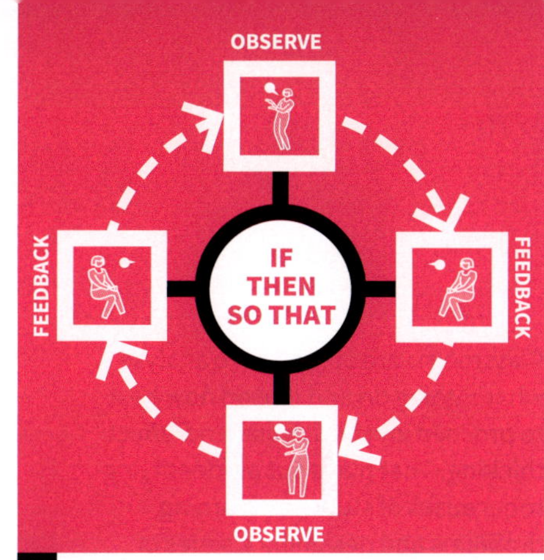

3

THEN…

Now agree on the teacher action that will drive the change. This should link directly to a concrete technique.

- …then I'll use **Cold Calling…**
- …then I'll use **Think, Pair, Share…**

This is the specific move the teacher will adapt and apply in the classroom. It's not a vague behaviour or hollow pledge, but a deliberate, purposeful action.

4

SO THAT…

Build a clear picture of what success looks like — what will this change look like for the students, and how will it support the teacher's practice?

- …so that when I ask a question, everybody thinks and formulates a response.
- …so that every student has a chance to rehearse and get feedback.

This final part grounds the goal in student learning and gives you something concrete to look for in the follow-up.

5

CARRY IT THROUGH

The goal is the lynchpin of the coaching cycle — it should stay front and centre when observing lessons, leading conversations and planning next steps. This keeps the focus on solving the problem, not just performing a routine. Don't move on until the goal is genuinely met. Refer back to it regularly to maintain focus.

In team coaching, check that everyone can clearly articulate the shared goal — it's what binds the collective effort together.

CAUSE & EFFECT THINKING

Classrooms are complex. To analyse what's going on and reason how best to proceed involves cause-and-effect thinking. That plays out as identifying root causes of students' learning problems and designing a series of actions to unblock the impediments to understanding. However, teacher thinking is mostly private and invisible. So a major task for a coach is to surface this thinking and make it explicit — the better to check its accuracy and utility — and then to create opportunities for it to develop in the process of designing teaching sequences to solve student learning problems.

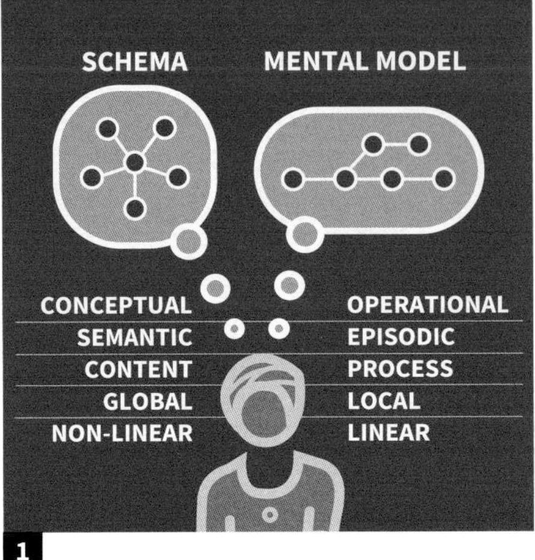

1

DISTINGUISH MENTAL MODELS FROM SCHEMAS

It's very useful to be clear about these two distinct, but overlapping, domains of understanding. Technical coaching focuses on the operational nature of mental models.

Unlike schemas, which center on what things are and their associated characteristics, mental models are procedural and operational, concerned with function and cause-and-effect relationships.

SHEILA PONTIS

2

BUILD YOUR MENTAL MODELS WITH SCRIPTS

Scripts is the term coined by cognitive scientist, Roger Schank, for our private mini-rules of how the world around us works. They help us map the familiar onto new, unfamiliar circumstances — famously exemplified by Schank's restaurant scenarios. A key job of coaching is to surface our usually private, unexamined scripts about teaching.

ROGER SCHANK

Scripts … make clear what is supposed to happen and what various acts on the part of others are supposed to indicate.

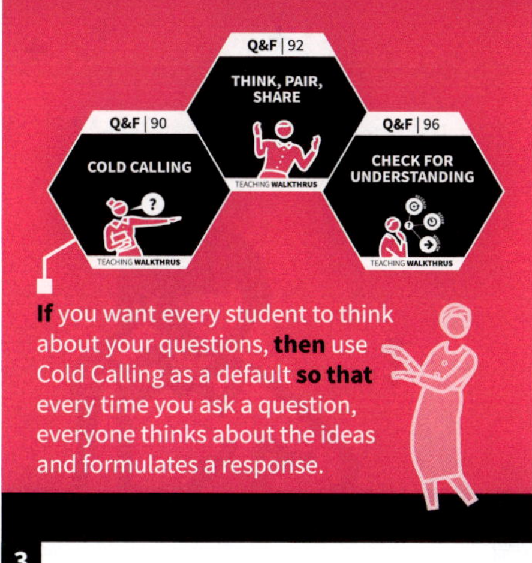

3

CREATE CAUSAL CHAINS WITH WALKTHRU CLUSTERS

A teacher's scripts surface in the process of constructing a WalkThru Cluster, through the reasoned sequencing of techniques into a fluent combination. In the process, the reasoning is subject to — and developed by — the logical discipline of the **If…Then…So That…** structure.

In dialogues such as these with a coach (or colleague), scripts and their assumptions are under joint exploration. When part of **Three-Point Communication**, the tone is set up to be consistent with a partnership approach to joint learning.

4

MAKE PREDICTIONS & LEARN FROM ANY ERRORS

Without forming a hypothesis, learning from experience is less likely to be meaningful. That's why cause-and-effect thinking is critical. Its end product is the predicted outcome of the intended teaching process. If accurate, it reinforces your initial thoughts; if not, it triggers a need for deep learning.

> Thoughts are intertwined with practice, so if we want to better understand practice, we need to also understand the thoughts that guide practice.

5

MAXIMISE THE COACHING OPPORTUNITY

The coach can play a pivotal role in revealing the cognitive component of teaching, all the while talking about its practicalities.

As teachers are with their coaches for only about 2% of their time, coaches need to decide how best to support the remaining 98%. That's where the cognitive approach pays dividends. However, beware of overplaying the cognitive approach at the expense of teaching techniques, as the topic risks becoming dry and abstract.

By co-creating WalkThru Clusters, coaches intertwine both dimensions to great effect.

FOCUS ON LEARNING: THREE CHECKS

It's important for coaching processes to focus on student learning as the ultimate goal for any teacher actions. Crucially, we mean all students; teachers need to plan for everyone in their class to be learning and to check that this is happening.

The emphasis on all is a central challenge for teaching, not least because we can't always tell if learning is happening, especially in a short observation. Three simple questions can help to unpack the complexity.

1

IS EVERYONE THINKING?

Cognitive science tells us that thinking is the key to learning. When teachers set tasks or ask questions, they should ensure all students have a chance to think for themselves. For example, **Cold Calling**, **Show-Me Boards** and **Show Call** all require each individual student to produce answers themselves; they all have to think. Coaching can explore the precision in each of these techniques.

2

IS EVERYONE MAKING MEANING?

Each student will need to make sense of the concepts and skills being taught for themselves.

In practical situations, this can be seen by observing students or looking at their work. In others, teachers need to elicit responses from students to check their understanding. **Check for Understanding, Think, Pair, Share**, **Practise Explaining** and **Modelling Handover** can be helpful techniques to explore.

3

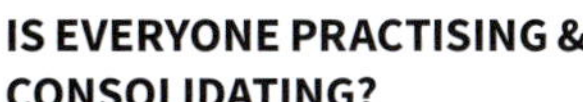

IS EVERYONE PRACTISING & CONSOLIDATING?

New learning is often very tenuous and will be forgotten rapidly unless students practise using the new learning to reinforce new connections and consolidate learning in their schema.

The most effective form of practice will vary so it's important to explore appropriate techniques adapted for the subject, such as **Guided Practice, Building Fluency** and **Independent Practice**.

4

LITERALLY EVERYONE? A POWERFUL REALITY CHECK

When teachers are in full flow, running the room, explaining and questioning, it is challenging to monitor the learning of each and every student.

A coach can support the teacher, checking whether any specific students are obviously opting out or overlooked or whether each student engages fully in paired talk. These insights can help develop techniques with precise student-focused action steps.

5

THREE SNAPSHOT CHECKS IN PRACTICE

Each of the three questions can inform rich coaching conversations over multiple cycles. However, during observations it's only realistic to make snapshot checks, related to the teacher's focus.

Scanning the class and listening in as a few pairs of students share ideas can reveal a sample of student interactions that merit discussion providing ample material to inform the coaching.

WALKTHRU **WHAT?** SERIES

TRAIN & MODEL

Training is an important but often overlooked part of effective coaching. Done well, it helps teachers understand not just what to do, but why it matters and how it works in real classrooms. Organised around our adaptation of Theory, See It, Name It, Do It, this series offers a set of practical WalkThrus for planning and delivering effective training, unpacking techniques and helping teachers build strong mental models for teaching through effective modelling.

THE TENNIS PLAYER ANALOGY

The Tennis Player Analogy helps highlight key aspects of instructional coaching.

Players strive for excellence in their performance; they use well-defined techniques and seek to improve through routine practice.

Coaches use their knowledge of the game to help players understand how to improve as well as providing motivational guidance.

1

COACHING CONTINUES FROM NOVICE TO EXPERT

Top-level players fully recognise the value of being coached and continually strive to improve the core techniques they use every match. Champion players don't complain that it's beneath them to focus on their serve or backhand as if they are too basic. These strokes are analogous to, say, **Cold Call** and **Think, Pair, Share** in teaching.

2

ROLES & RELATIONSHIPS

A tennis coach observes the player play to gain insights into their strengths and areas to work on. You can't coach by sitting in the dressing room. Coaches then work with the player to plan appropriate practice tasks.

Coaching can be directive but the focus is always on the player's sense of their physical actions, mindset and decision-making.

3

CORE TECHNIQUES; CREATIVE PLAYERS

Tennis is played using a set of techniques that are well understood among all players. They can be codifed and practised in isolation.

However, tennis players are still highly individual in style — they use techniques creatively to express themselves on the court. Here, as in teaching, creativity builds on sound technique.

4

PRACTICE & PERFORMANCE

Tennis practice focuses on repeating certain specific skills to build up a level of fluency. Then, in a game scenario, the players attempt to apply the skills they've practised in response to their opponent.

To improve their performance, they don't just play more matches — they break things down to focus their practice on specific skills, guided by their coach.

5

RESPONSIVE COMBINATIONS

Every tennis player will learn to serve, volley and use their forehand and backhand. However, these skills are not very effective on their own; it is the way they are combined, responding to the opponent's shots, that determines their impact.

This is analogous to Clusters of WalkThrus: techniques often work better in combination than by themselves.

EVERY TEACHER THINKING

Training is such a crucial part of the coaching process, so it's important that everyone sees it as serious professional work. That means more than just turning up — it means everyone thinking hard, participating fully and taking it seriously.

To make that happen, we need to create the right conditions. High-participation workshops don't happen by accident — they need to be planned properly and well led by coaches who are knowledgable and confident. When teachers think deeply during training, they're far more likely to apply what they've learned where it matters — in the classroom.

1

GIVE IT STATUS

Training should feel like professional work, not an add-on. Set clear expectations — be on time, be present, be engaged.

Don't let staff room habits creep in. No marking, no emails. Use agreed protocols to keep the focus on high-quality thinking and discussion.

2

MAKE IT RELEVANT

Teachers switch off when training feels disconnected from their practice. Use real classroom content, not gimmicky examples. If coaching a mixed group, acknowledge different contexts — subject, phase and year group matter. Frame ideas through authentic curriculum content so every teacher sees the value.

3

INVOLVE EVERYONE

Run training with high-participation routines — **Think, Pair, Share**, peer-supported rehearsal and structured discussion. This isn't just engagement; it's ensuring everyone is actively thinking.

Watch for those sitting back. Everyone thinks, everyone contributes. Done well, this builds energy, focus and a shared sense of purpose.

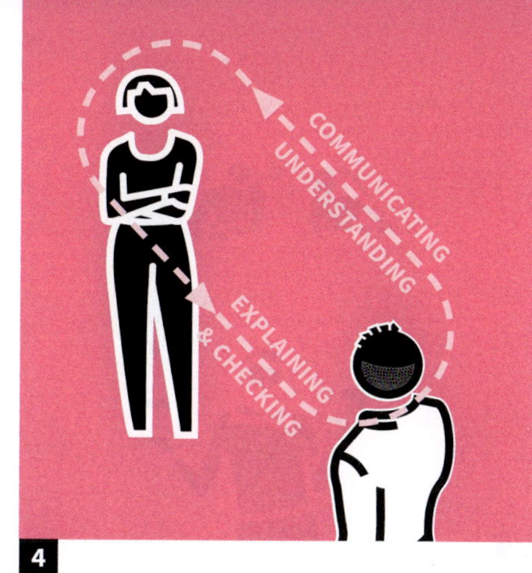

4

CHECK FOR UNDERSTANDING

Every teacher should leave with a clear, accurate understanding of the technique — its purpose, when to use it and common pitfalls.

Check for understanding frequently, but avoid weak proxies like thumbs up/down. Get real evidence — listen to discussions, use **Cold Call** question routines and ensure everyone *gets it* before they leave.

5

PRODUCE A CONCRETE OUTCOME

Every teacher should leave with something tangible — an annotated technique, a scripted example, a rollout plan or a personal goal on a Post-it note.

This isn't about evidence collection. It's about focusing attention and clarifying next steps. A concrete outcome helps both teacher and coach see what's needed for success.

THEORY, SEE IT, NAME IT, DO IT

In *Teaching WalkThrus 3*, we featured Leila MacTavish's adaptation of Bambrick-Santoyo's *See It, Name It, Do It* framework. As our coaching approach has developed, the **Theory, See It, Name It, Do It** model has become more prominent in our thinking. Applied as a structure for training workshops, it is the perfect vehicle to deliver the active ingredients needed to develop teachers' schema and build strong mental models of teaching: knowledge, modelling, technique and rehearsal.

1

THEORY

Teacher motivation is key to their success in training. Convince participants of the importance of the work by drawing on theory and research, highlighting the impact on children's learning. Select from the strategies in **Theory | The Cognitive Argument:**

- The Learning Model.
- A-B scenarios.
- Head-on misconceptions.
- Guided goal reflection.
- Debate and disagreement.

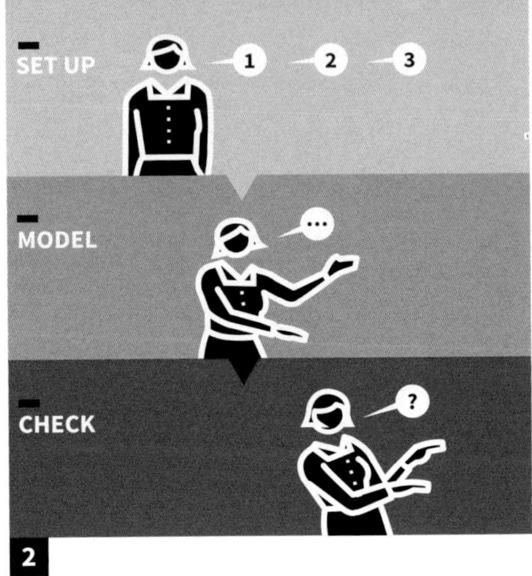

2

SEE IT

Provide teachers with concrete examples of the target technique. Use representations of effective practice alongside non-examples. The important thing is to carefully guide teachers' deconstruction and analysis of the model, making visible the characteristics that make it more and less effective and when.

Apply the **Principles of Modelling** to your planning, and remember that different techniques can be modelled in different ways. Match the technique with the strategies suggested in **See It | Ways of Modelling.**

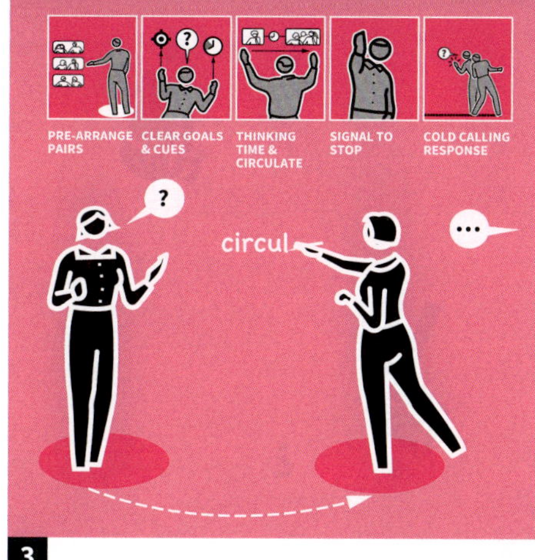

3

NAME IT

Build teachers' deep understanding of the technique by breaking it down into its constituent parts in order to surface the components that make it effective. Playbook techniques are provisional until they are made concrete by the teacher, first by decomposing the practice to reveal its secrets, then recomposing in the form of their own specific context.

This process is explored in the WalkThru **Name It | Decomposition, Recomposition**. Crucial to this is our concept of **A|D|A|P|T**, which you can find in the **Adapt & Apply** chapter.

4

DO IT

Provide opportunities for purposeful rehearsal. This is the core step in setting in motion the functional dynamic between knowing (schema) and doing (mental models). Rehearsal doesn't mean role play; it means finding meaningful ways to approximate the practice and get feedback in order to build lesson-readiness. This can start in the training room and continue in the classroom.

We'll explore this aspect in more detail in the **Adapt & Apply** chapter.

5

INCLUDE ALL ELEMENTS

The **Theory, See It, Name It, Do It** structure works because it makes space for the instructional pedagogies that support transfer (see **Representation, Decomposition & Approximation**). You need to include all elements.

As a guide, allocate 25% of the available time to each part. It's natural that classroom rehearsal will follow in the **Adapt & Apply** phase, but it's important to get the ball rolling in the training room. The WalkThrus in this section give you specific strategies to use.

THEORY | THE COGNITIVE ARGUMENT

As we explore in **Meaningful Coaching**, teachers commit to change when it feels relevant and worthwhile. This starts with a deep understanding of the problem they are trying to solve and a recognition of how the solution might impact on student learning in their classroom.

This WalkThru suggests five ways that coaches can convince teachers of the cognitive argument: the rationale that underpins the importance of the work.

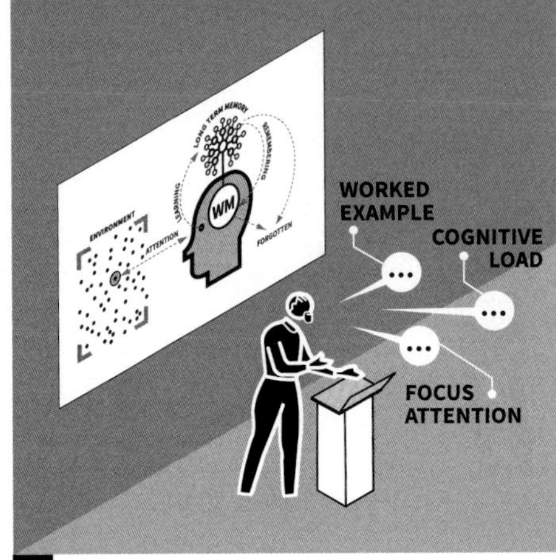

1

THE LEARNING MODEL

In our training, we start with **The Learning Model**. It's a useful stimulus for developing a shared understanding of the learning problem we are trying to solve and why the solution we have designed might be effective. For example, training on **Worked Examples** might start with a consideration of the potential cognitive benefits: reducing cognitive load/focusing attention on key features/prompting deep thinking. Ideally, teachers will be familiar enough with **The Learning Model** to generate a list of benefits; if not, share them and allow some focused time for discussion before moving on.

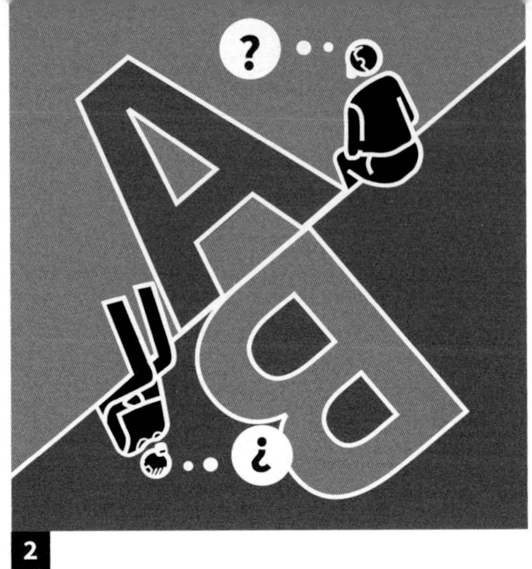

2

A-B SCENARIOS

Present two contrasting futures — one where the target technique hasn't yet been adopted (A) and one where it is well embedded (B). Make it concrete and classroom-focused:

SCENARIO A | 'In this classroom, thinking is optional. Students opt out easily, and discussion is dominated by just one or two.'

SCENARIO B | 'In this classroom, everybody is thinking. Every student has time to formulate their response. Every student contributes to the lesson.'

CHOICE | 'Which classroom would you rather have? Why?' Use the contrast to create urgency and motivation.

3

HEAD-ON MISCONCEPTIONS

Expose and unpick any lingering misconceptions that teachers might hold about the target technique.

ANTICIPATE | 'Cold Calling is just no hands up.' / 'Students learn best when they choose their own talk-partners.'

CHALLENGE | 'Why is this so widely believed?' / 'What's the flaw in this logic?'

REBUILD | Clarify the correct model using evidence and practical examples.

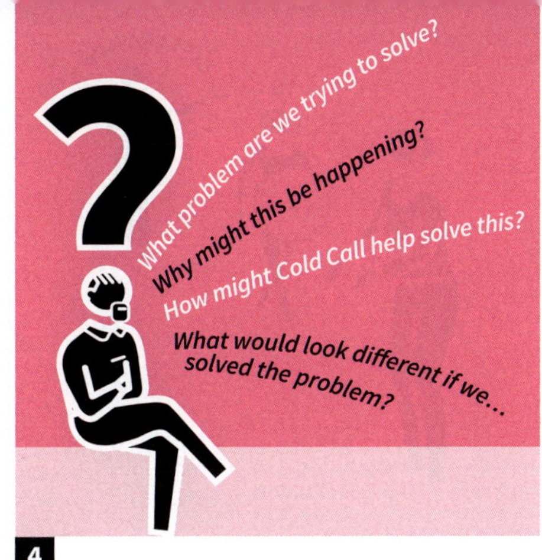

4

GUIDED GOAL REFLECTION

Guide teachers through the **If... Then... So That...** goal using direct, specific questions:

- 'What problem are we trying to solve here?'
- 'Why might this be happening?'
- 'How might [technique] help to solve this?'
- 'What would look different if we solved the problem?'

Prompt each teacher to take ownership by stating (or jotting down) an individual commitment to action.

5

DEBATE & DISAGREEMENT

Create a structured discussion where teachers can unpick the rationale behind the work expected of them. If they harbour reservations, they won't invest in making it happen. Invite debate and challenge:

- 'Why might this not work?'
- 'What concerns you about this approach?'
- 'Are we missing anything here?'

Run the discussion in a way that values opinions, even if you don't agree with what is said. It's worth addressing these concerns now before they become barriers later.

SEE IT | PRINCIPLES OF MODELLING

Models — or representations of practice — help teachers to build a clear picture of a teaching technique, making it more likely that they will be able to enact it effectively in their own classroom.

Coaches use models to make visible the core characteristics of the technique and to surface the intentional thinking underpinning when, how and why the technique might be used. While this WalkThru explores the principles of effective modelling, you can explore different strategies in **See It | Ways of Modelling**.

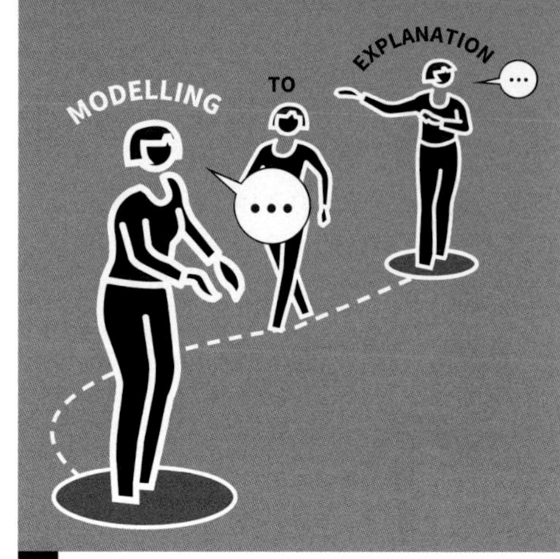

1

MAKE TIME FOR PURPOSEFUL MODELLING

The *Education Endowment Foundation's* 2022 guidance report identifies modelling as a core mechanism of effective PD. Yet, due to time constraints or a lack of confidence from the coach, models are often left out of training workshops.

Prioritise time to deliver, deconstruct and analyse multiple models. Don't feel nervous about modelling; you instantly gain credibility by practising what you preach. And remember that different techniques can be modelled in different ways; it doesn't necessarily need to be all eyes on you.

2

PRESENT MODELS OF MORE & LESS EFFECTIVE PRACTICE

Provide models of the technique done well alongside non-examples — models where the technique has been intentionally problematised. For example, live model a **Cold Call** routine where the teacher is strategic about which student they invite to answer. Then, live model a **Cold Call** routine where student selection is randomised.

Examining the difference between examples and non-examples in this way demonstrates the breadth and boundaries of the concept being trained. Ideally, you'll run this routine several times — one model is rarely sufficient.

3

PRESENT MODELS FROM RELEVANT CONTEXTS

As we explore in **Every Teacher Thinking**, teachers switch off when training feels disconnected from their practice. If a model feels unfamiliar, they won't see themselves ever using the technique.

Use examples that reflect the settings they work in — different curriculum areas, year groups and phases. Use real classroom content, not gimmicky examples. Be cautious with video models from other schools — if the context feels too distant, it can become a distraction rather than a useful reference.

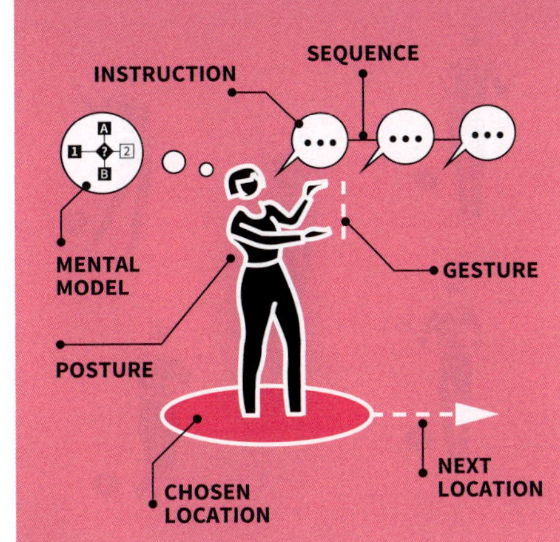

4

GUIDE DECONSTRUCTION & ANALYSIS

Don't assume that teachers will recognise the mechanisms of a technique just by observing it. Before expecting them to analyse or adopt it, break it down into its core parts, highlighting important features to make them visible. For example:

- The specific language aspects that make a **Cold Call** question invitational rather than imposing.
- The use of metacognitive narration in a **Worked Example**.

Guided deconstruction and analysis increase the likelihood that everyone is thinking about the right thing at the right time.

5

CHECK FOR UNDERSTANDING

As you present, deconstruct and analyse models, introduce frequent checks for understanding. Every teacher should leave with a confident, accurate understanding of the technique — its key features, its purpose, its limitations.

Use short feedback loops, allowing time for discussion as and when important features are made visible. Don't race through the model assuming everyone is keeping up — pause regularly to check understanding and respond to any uncertainty.

SEE IT | WAYS OF MODELLING

Some techniques — such as behaviour routines, questions or paired-talk structures — are best modelled live in the training room. Others, like explanations, may be better explored through scripts, transcripts or video analysis.

The key is to match the technique to the most effective modelling method, using the **Principles of Modelling** to make its core features visible and ensure teachers develop a clear understanding.

1

LIVE MODELS

Model techniques live in the training room, allowing teachers to see them enacted in real time. Demonstrate the technique confidently and professionally, avoiding the temptation to overact or play up to your peers — the goal is to demonstrate the technique as it should look in the classroom. As you model, narrate your actions explicitly, explaining what you are doing and why, but without disrupting the fluency of the demonstration. Follow up with guided deconstruction and analysis, checking that teachers have understood the key features and intentional decisions behind the model.

2

VISUAL INSTRUCTIONS

Visual instructions that use both words and static images (like our WalkThrus!) offer clear and concise models of expert pedagogy. Chip and Dan Heath report that reading and imagining yourself performing selected actions later on improves actual performance.

Encourage teachers to visualise themselves performing each step as they work through the model. Prompt them to build a mental image of each step in their own classroom setting. Have them talk through the sequence aloud, either to you or a peer, to reinforce clarity and retention.

3

VIDEO MODELS

Video models are useful but must be carefully selected. Ideally, build an in-house video library — teachers benefit more from seeing techniques applied in their own context with their own students.

Play the video through once in real time; keep clips short and focused. Replay with pauses at key moments to guide deconstruction and analysis. Prepare multiple examples, including non-examples, so teachers can compare more effective and less effective characteristics.

4

SCRIPTS & TRANSCRIPTS

Dialogic techniques — such as explaining or questioning — can be modelled using scripts or transcripts. For example:

- Use a scripted explanation of a relevant concept and have teachers analyse its features (key terms/narrative structure/ concrete examples).
- Guide teachers in breaking down a transcript of a classroom Q&A exchange, focusing on important characteristics (question stem/thinking time/student responses).

Situate the analysis within a clear purpose — teachers should identify the effective features.

5

CO-OBSERVATION & CO-TEACHING

Some techniques are best modelled in a classroom rather than a training room:

CO-OBSERVATION | WATCHING ANOTHER TEACHER | Sit alongside the teacher and guide their attention to key features that might otherwise be missed. Avoid disrupting the observed lesson or putting pressure on the teacher to *perform*.

CO-TEACHING | Works best where the coach has direct expertise in the approach being developed. Work together to plan the model, checking that the why is clearly understood. Support without taking over; the teacher must remain the authority in their classroom.

NAME IT | DECOMPOSITION, RECOMPOSITION

Building on Pam Grossman's work, research from Ambition Institute (Banks et al., 2024) shows that coaches should combine decomposition and recomposition to help teachers understand not just how a technique works, but when to use it.

Decomposition breaks a technique into steps to make its most important features visible. Recomposition rebuilds the steps into a more meaningful whole; a technique adapted for the teacher's classroom. This combination sharpens teachers' understanding of a technique and bridges the gap between the **Train & Model** and **Adapt & Apply** stages of the coaching process.

1

NAME THE STEPS

Break the technique into steps, making its core parts visible. Form a sequence — a series of individual moves with a start, middle and end. This is how our WalkThrus are designed. Name each step to build a shared language that allows you to unpack the technique and talk about it in a cohesive way.

A well-structured breakdown removes uncertainty, helping teachers understand what to do, when to do it and why it matters.

2

EXAMINE KEY ASPECTS

Break each step down deliberately — don't assume teachers will notice the key features on their own. Guide their thinking by highlighting why each step matters, how it works and when to use it. Focus on the nuance of execution — e.g. specific cues, timings, language features or checks.

Teachers should fully understand the mechanisms that make the technique effective before moving on. Secure understanding first — then build on it.

3

MODEL IN ISOLATION

If a teacher struggles with a specific step, model or re-model it in isolation to build clarity before returning to the full sequence. Complex steps may need to be modelled at a smaller grain size to secure understanding. For example, if a teacher is unsure what it means to ask a question aimed at everyone in the room, focus on modelling question stems rather than an entire questioning routine.

4

REBUILD USING A|D|A|P|T

Breaking a technique into steps is useful, but without recomposition, teachers can struggle to see how it fits into real classroom practice. Use the **A|D|A|P|T Framework** to structure the rebuild, helping the teacher to situate the steps within their own specific context.

Adapting the technique to make it more meaningful builds a much clearer understanding of how it can be used at the right time, for the right reason.

5

REHEARSE IN MEANINGFUL CONTEXTS

Teachers need to practise their adapted techniques properly — first in the training room, then in the classroom. Make the rehearsal as close to real life as possible.

Give precise feedback so they can adjust and improve quickly. Use the **Adapt & Apply** WalkThrus to support this process and ensure the technique is embedded.

WORKED EXAMPLE | COLD CALLING

In our training programmes we always include **Cold Calling** early on because it is such a powerful, inclusive technique that teachers can use every lesson, every day.

The goal of the training is to support teachers to make sense of the ideas for themselves, recognising the habits they currently have and leaving with a plan of action for the changes they need to make. By acting out a full **Cold Calling** sequence in the session, it creates a vivid reference for teachers' own mental models and the issues can be explored in detail.

1

THEORY | SET UP CLASS SCENARIO; EXPLORE RATIONALE

Establish that you will run the training room like a classroom. You'll ask some questions using **Cold Calling** and, therefore, every participant should expect to be asked for their answers.

The rationale is that, in doing this, it helps them all to:

- Focus their attention and generate thinking.
- Retrieve relevant information and rehearse answers.

It also provides assessment information to the teacher.

2

SEE IT | ENACT ALL FIVE STEPS WITH PRECISION

Use the stem: *OK, everyone, have a think....* then pose the question.

Our go-to question is: *What are all the colours the sky can be and when do you see them?*

This works because a) everyone knows some answers, and b) its structure allows scope for follow-up questions.

- Give thinking time — make it silent.
- Select someone to respond and follow up: *Red, orange and pink? Lovely choices — and when would you see a pink sky?*
- Repeat with at least one more person.

3

NAME IT | INVITE TEACHERS TO REHEARSE THEIR MODEL

Now remove visuals showing the WalkThru and invite participants to run through and share their recall of each of the five steps in pairs.

This makes everyone explore their personal mental model:

- Do they have a clear sense of the sequence?
- Did they miss out any vital part?

Show the WalkThru on a slide so everyone can compare with the version they generated. Reinforce the value of each step and problems that arise if they are missed.

4

IDENTIFY BARRIERS & PITFALLS

Explore concerns and doubts, because unless teachers are comfortable with the ideas, they're very unlikely to apply them to their lessons. In pairs, invite participants to discuss any issues that might emerge with **Cold Calling**. Gather some responses which may include:

- How to include someone who is anxious or shy?
- What if someone is wrong or says 'I don't know' as a default?

Prepare for and field these queries with reference to **Cold Call Variations, No Opt Out** or **Say It Again Better**.

5

A|D|A|P|T & PLAN THE PRACTICE

To transfer the ideas from the training room into each teacher's practice, ask them to explore the **A|D|A|P|T** process:

- Plan specific lessons and exact questions they might ask with **Cold Calling**.
- Plan opening stems that invite everyone to think – e.g. 'Right, everyone thinking please... What is ...?'
- Plan responses to 'I don't know' – e.g. 'OK, you're not sure: what question did I ask you?'

Invite everyone to highlight the one key step they will take to develop their **Cold Calling** in the coming week.

ADAPT & APPLY

The Adapt & Apply series provides a set of WalkThrus designed to help coaches support teachers in using techniques effectively in their own classrooms. Our A|D|A|P|T concept — which features heavily in our *Teaching WalkThrus* series — is central here, offering a clear structure for adapting and embedding techniques in context. The collection also includes practical guidance on facilitating effective rehearsal, supporting classroom implementation, and using drop-ins as a formative tool to gather insights and guide next steps.

DO IT | ADAPT

We introduced the **A|D|A|P|T** acronym in our *Teaching WalkThrus* books to emphasise the importance of teachers needing to assimilate ideas into their own schema, appropriate for their contexts. WalkThrus are an attempt to codify and simplify common teaching techniques — but they are not fixed rules to abide by. They can't be a rigid checklist. The A|D|A|P|T approach can support everyone in a coaching dialogue to move towards teachers forming better habits that make an impact on learning.

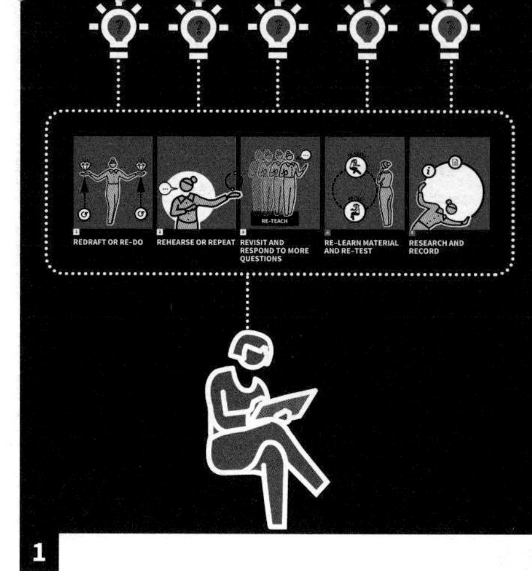

1

ATTEMPT

Very obviously, perhaps, we don't get better at things we never try! However, making an attempt to use a new approach can actually be the hardest part. Inertia and resistance to change are strong. If we make it low stakes — just a case of giving something a go to see what happens — it's more likely teachers will try things out. Creating that culture should be a goal for coaching.

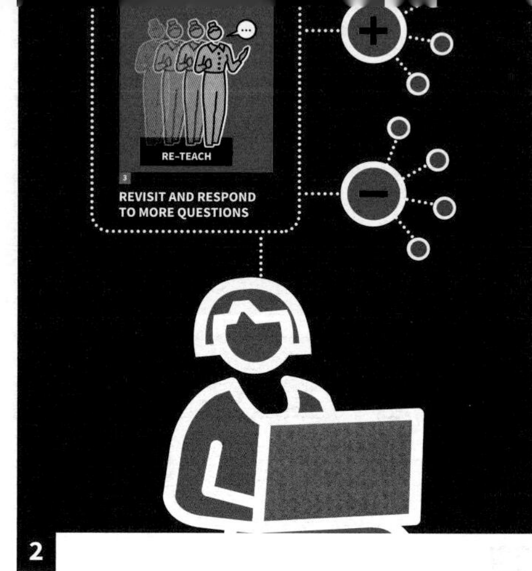

2

DEVELOP

Here, the idea is to flesh out the rough outline the WalkThrus provide by adding details and subtle variations. For example, with any questioning technique, the actual specific questions we ask and how they are structured needs development. The exact rules we devise with **Establish Your Expectations** or the signal we use in **Signal, Pause, Insist** need to be specific to the class context.

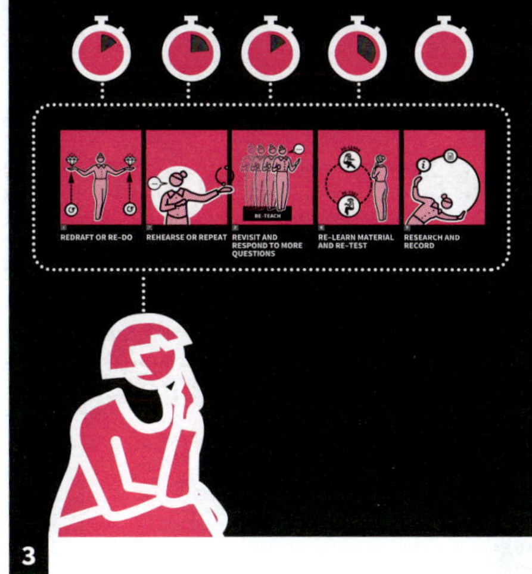

ADAPT

Teachers might adapt an approach to make it work with their subject or class — e.g. with some children, when using **Cold Calling**, an adaptation might be for them to write down their thoughts before sharing them. **Cold Call Variations** explores other similar ideas. **Live Modelling**, which appears to describe a classroom context, will need to be adapted for the sports field or the drama studio, even if the basic ideas transfer.

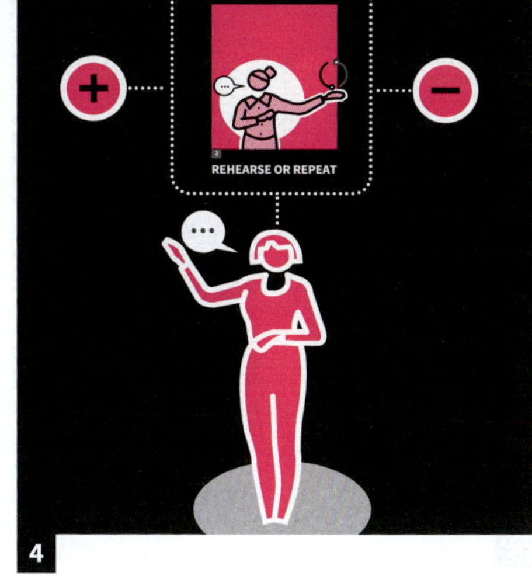

4

PRACTISE

When teachers try new techniques and find that they don't work smoothly, feeling awkward or taking up time, often it's simply a case of needing to practise them so that they flow more fluently. This requires practice. If an approach is identified as a good solution to a problem, it pays to practise it over some time before evaluating its impact. Coaches can provide important encouragement to persist.

5

TEST

Finally, discuss how a teacher will know if their approach is working:

- What will it look like if you've been successful?
- What mental criteria do you have to judge that behaviour or student work is *excellent*?

If the test suggests that the impact isn't sufficient, it could be that further developments or adapations are needed alongside more practice.

DO IT | TRAINING ROOM REHEARSAL

The EEF (2021) identifies rehearsal as a core mechanism of effective professional development. Practising a technique at least once outside the classroom helps teachers refine their skills and embed habits before applying them in real lessons. Rehearsing away from classroom pressures — with the support of a peer or coach — allows teachers to practise, adapt and build confidence.

In this WalkThru, we explore structured rehearsal methods that help teachers refine techniques in a controlled setting before taking them into the classroom.

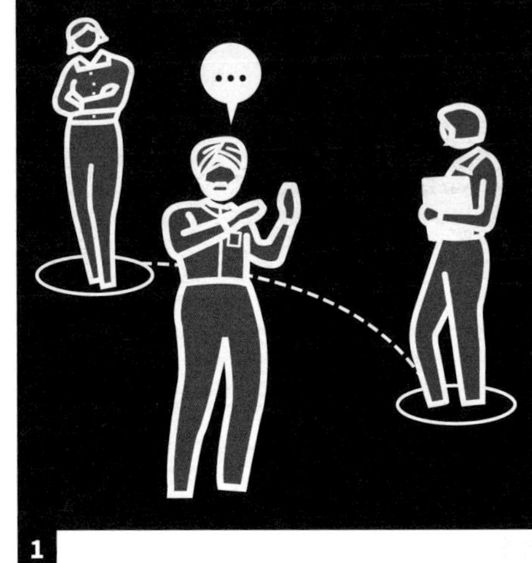

1

PEER-SUPPORTED REHEARSAL

Get teachers practising immediately in pairs or small groups to build fluency and confidence. Mix part-rehearsal (practising a single step) and whole-rehearsal (practising the entire technique).

Use short feedback loops so adjustments can be made and tested in real time. Feedback must be tightly focused on the teacher's recomposed technique — no drift. Draw a clear line between rehearsal and role-play. This isn't about acting out a part; it's about approximating real practice in a meaningful context.

2

SCRIPTING

Techniques with dialogic elements can be scripted in the training room, such as:

- Metacognitive narration for a **Worked Example**.
- An explanation of a difficult concept.
- A question for a **Think, Pair, Share** routine.

Scripts should be clear, concise and curriculum-based, written word for word. Teachers annotate their scripts, thinking through their design decisions. They should talk through their script with a peer or coach, making quick, targeted adjustments based on feedback. Once rehearsal is complete, the script serves as a prompt in the classroom, helping to reinforce the teacher's new habit.

3

COGNITIVE REHEARSAL

Research shows that mentally rehearsing a situation helps us perform better when we encounter that situation in the physical environment.

Have teachers mentally walk through each step of the technique, thinking through what they will do, what they will say and how.

CHIP & DAN HEATH

Sitting quietly, without moving, and picturing yourself performing a task successfully from start to finish — improves performance significantly.

4

VIDEO SELF-OBSERVATION

As Jim Knight says, video is rocket fuel for learning. Video helps teachers see their teaching as it really happens, not how they assume it does. Have them record short, focused clips (5-10 minutes) targeting a specific step or sequence. They should watch twice: once in real time, then with pauses to zoom in and reflect. Where possible, do this alongside a coach or peer — a second pair of eyes can be helpful. To close the loop, they should plan the reshoot, making adjustments that nudge them closer to their goal.

5

SOLO REHEARSAL

Solo rehearsal allows teachers to practise a technique independently, without an audience, before using it in the classroom. They should rehearse with real curriculum content, either in front of a mirror, in an empty room or on video.

Encourage them to perform the technique exactly as they would in class, working one step at a time and thinking carefully about why and how they are doing it.

Keep it focused and iterative: short, targeted run-throughs, immediate adjustments and quick reattempts.

CLASSROOM REHEARSAL

Rehearsal starts in the training room, but it must continue in the classroom. It's match practice — building confidence and fluency in real conditions.

This WalkThru outlines five techniques for classroom rehearsal, helping teachers refine and embed techniques in real time. Teachers can apply these independently, but feedback from a coach or peer strengthens the process.

1

STAGGERED STEPS

Practise one step at a time, repeating it until fluent before adding the next. Changing too much at once leads to inconsistency. Isolate, refine and embed each step through repetition before moving forward. Fluency first, then depth.

SHOW-ME BOARDS | First, the teacher rehearses setting a question with thinking time. Once fluent, they introduce show-me routines, then refine how they sample responses.

2

UNSEEN SELF-OBSERVATION

Take structured notes immediately after teaching, but wait before reviewing. Reflecting too soon can reinforce assumptions rather than reveal insights. Leave at least 24 hours before analysing, ensuring a fresh perspective. Focus on a specifc step or sequence — not everything at once. Look for patterns, refine details and plan a single, targeted change for the next lesson.

SIGNAL, PAUSE, INSIST | The teacher reflects on how successful students were in offering their attention. The next day, they assess whether students responded immediately or whether they needed extra prompting.

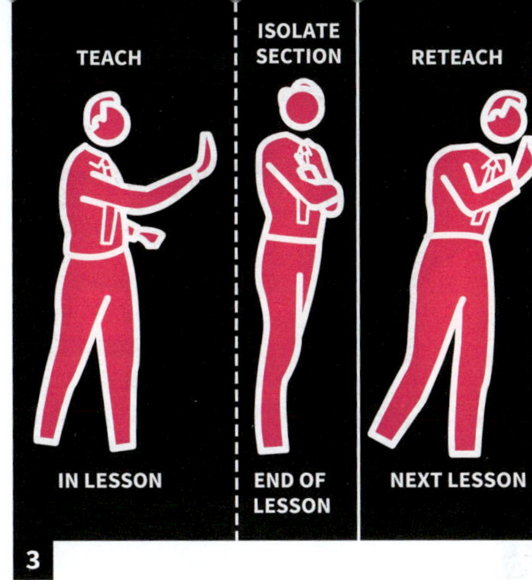

3

REPLAY & REFINE

Reteach a key moment immediately after the lesson, either alone or with your next class. Isolate the section, make an intentional change and repeat. Keep it short and focused — this is not a full lesson reset but a chance to refine a single step while it's still fresh. Adjust, repeat, improve.

CHORAL RESPONSE | Student responses were too quiet. The teacher practises mixing choral and individual responses so that students anticipate this and engage more fully.

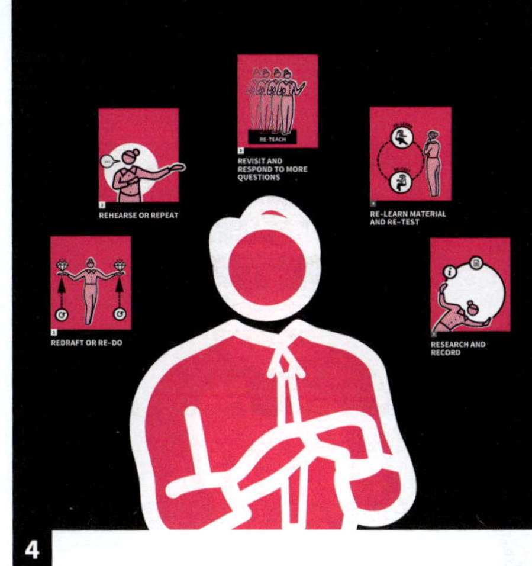

4

SELF-PROMPTING

Use structured cues to keep key adjustments front of mind during lessons. Identify common errors, then develop personal reminders — a sticky note, a hand signal or a silent self-check. Rehearse with prompts until adjustments become automatic. Remove cues gradually as fluency builds. Use the steps in **Prompts, Cues & Checklists** to help.

LIVE MODELLING | To reinforce *Organise messy thinking*, the teacher writes 'Think aloud' on their whiteboard as a self-cue.

5

LIVE COACHING

Live coaching happens in the classroom, in real time. You're in the room, giving immediate, in-lesson feedback to help the teacher refine their technique on the spot.

But it only works if the culture is right — you're there to support, not undermine. Guide teachers with non-verbal cues, quiet prompts or quick resets, keeping your involvement minimal and precise. If needed, briefly model before stepping back.

After the lesson, run a quick debrief to check for understanding and reinforce the changes.

ROUTINE BUILDING

In *Teach Like a Champion*, Doug Lemov emphasises that a new technique only becomes a tool for success when it becomes habit. Routines don't just happen — they must be built. A key challenge in the **Adapt & Apply** stage is embedding the technique meaningfully in the teacher's classroom.

Help teachers install a routine around the technique. A rushed rollout leads to confusion, inconsistency and wasted time. A precise rollout ensures teachers practise with intention, build fluency and make the technique a permanent part of their teaching.

DOUG LEMOV

1

PLAN THE ROLLOUT

A rollout is a short, clear explanation where the teacher introduces the routine and its purpose to students. Support teachers in scripting exactly what they will say — it should be crisp, direct and honest.
For example: 'When I ask a question, it's for everyone. No calling out, no hands up. In silence, so that everybody can think hard.'

Help teachers define exactly what they expect students to do and why it matters. Name the routine — e.g. **Cold Calling** or **Everybody Thinking** — to make it easy for students to remember.

2

OUTLINE THE STEPS

Help teachers break the routine into an explicit sequence that students can follow. For **Cold Calling**, this might be:

- Listen to the question.
- Think in silence.
- No hands up.
- Listen, build and challenge.

Check that students understand the cues that trigger each step, not just the routine itself. They need to know what to do, when to do it and how to do it well.

3

MODEL & DESCRIBE

Before running the routine for the first time, the teacher must explain and show students how to do it. Support them in delivering a clear, confident model, demonstrating each step exactly as expected.

Walk students through the routine, assessing how each step lands, and repeating until the standard is set. If expectations aren't high from the start, they'll be harder to enforce later.

4

PRACTISE

Routines must be practised until automatic. If details slip, expectations drop, and students lose clarity on what's expected. For example, allowing one student to call out an answer can quickly escalate and derail the routine.

Practice isn't just repetition — it's about getting it right every time. Support teachers in structuring a rehearsal phase where students practise under close observation. Reinforce what's correct and correct what isn't immediately before bad habits form. One good run-through isn't enough — keep practising until it's consistent.

5

TRANSFER OWNERSHIP

A routine isn't embedded in one lesson — it must be reinforced until automatic. Help teachers plan how they will monitor, reinforce and correct the routine over time. Anticipate enforcement fatigue. When a routine starts to slip, teachers need a plan to reboot it. Support them in re-explaining, re-modelling and re-practising so students reconnect with expectations.

A routine is a shared responsibility — teachers set and uphold expectations, but students must own their role in maintaining them. A routine only becomes a habit if it is relentlessly reinforced.

DROP-INS

Drop-ins are short, formative check-ins that help teachers refine a technique as they work towards their goal. By this stage, the teacher has already identified what they are developing. Drop-ins serve two purposes:

- Gather focused insights on how thetechnique is being used and its effect on students.
- Identify patterns to shape individual or team-based coaching.

The focus is on refinement, not evaluation. The goal is to collect useful insights that help teachers sharpen their use of the focal technique. The WalkThrus in **Diagnose & Design** will support this process.

1

DROP IN

Spend 5-10 minutes in the classroom, concentrating only on the agreed-upon technique. Use the guidance in **Building Trust** to ensure everyone understands the purpose. Avoid assessing everything — your job is to home in on how the technique is applied and its impact on students. Drop-ins can be prearranged if the teacher plans to use the technique at a specific moment, but they should still feel natural, not staged. The goal is to see real classroom practice, not a performance. Be sensible about timing — you're unlikely to see **Live Modelling** in the final minutes of a lesson.

2

SPOTLIGHT NOT FLOODLIGHT

Drop-ins require a spotlight lens. You're not scanning everything, you're locking in on how the teacher's adapted technique is applied and whether it's moving them towards meeting their goal.

For example, if the goal is: 'If you want all students to think about your questions, then use **Cold Calling** so that every student formulates a response.'

Then, **Cold Call** is the focus. Did the teacher follow the steps as designed, at the right time and for the right reason? How many students formulated a response, and how do we know? Keep the spotlight on what matters.

COLLECT INSIGHTS

Not every drop-in will capture the technique exactly as expected. Some techniques unfold over time, not in a single moment. If it's not immediately visible, don't force it — avoid creating a performance culture where teachers feel pressured to showcase techniques just because you've arrived at the door. Instead, collect relevant insights that still inform the teacher's goal. Shift the focus from what the teacher is doing to what students are doing. Even if the technique isn't visible, gathering useful observations ensures the drop-in remains aligned with the goal and focused on learning.

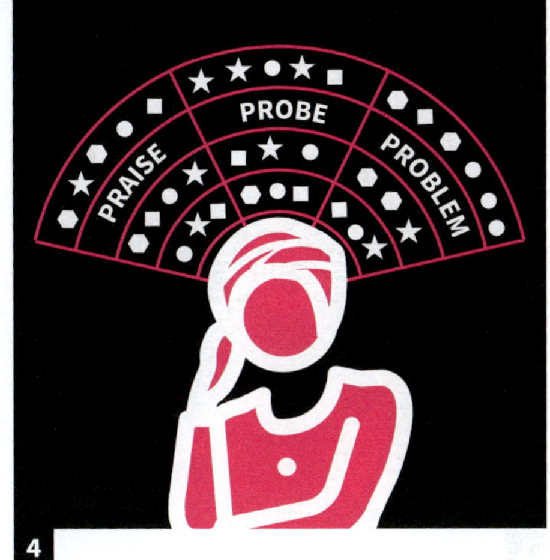

ORGANISE YOUR THINKING

Take time to make sense of what you've seen. Use **The 5Ps Framework**, focusing on the first three steps:

PRAISE | Affirm elements of the technique that are working.

PROBE | Identify what hasn't yet landed and explore why.

PROBLEM | Pinpoint the sticking point and next steps.

Use insights from the drop-in to help you plan for the **Feedback & Support** stage.

TEAM DROP-INS

When drop-ins are part of a team-based coaching cycle, the goal isn't individual feedback — it's gathering insights to inform the team conversation in the **Feedback & Support** stage. Be precise. Collect reliable, descriptive observations linked to the team goal, not vague impressions.

Look for patterns across classrooms to identify common challenges and opportunities that matter to everyone. Your unique perspective, having seen multiple lessons, allows you to steer the discussion towards important areas for improvement — focus on what'll make the biggest impact to the team.

SELF-MONITORING

Because teachers spend so much time on their own, it's useful to have a system for keeping track of how well a new technique is working.

Once they return to the busyness of the classroom, it's harder to stick with a habit change. Self-monitoring isn't about vague reflection or general self-evaluation. It's a sharp, practical process that helps teachers notice, review and adjust specific actions in the moment.

Use this as part of the **Adapt & Apply** phase to build a teacher's capacity to self-regulate and embed the technique with increasing independence.

1

PLAN

Help the teacher identify one precise, observable element of the technique to monitor. Keep it narrow and tied to a clear instructional intention. Avoid vague goals like 'use more **Cold Call**'. Instead: 'In a **Cold Call**, select at least three students to respond.'

Teachers can rehearse the action mentally or script examples to help them get lesson- ready. Define what counts and what doesn't. This primes attention and sets up purposeful noticing.

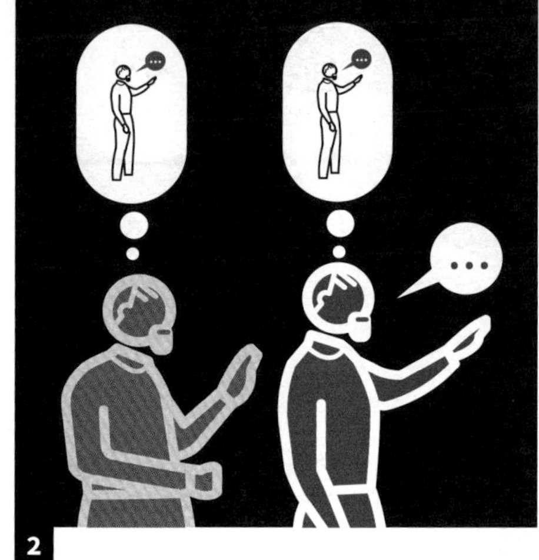

2

TEACH

The teacher delivers the lesson, focusing intentionally on the rehearsed action. It's a challenge in a real classroom, but the key is to hold the idea in working memory throughout the lesson.

It might be helpful to embed cues into lesson materials — slides, seating plans, Post-it notes — to help keep the action in mind during instruction. See **Prompts, Cues & Checklists**.

This builds reflection-in-action: the ability to monitor one's own actions in the moment while responding to the flow of the lesson.

3

TRACK

Introduce a simple, low-interference method for the teacher to track their actions during the lesson. This might include tally marks, visual prompts, cue cards or self-check reminders at key moments.

For example, tally the number of students involved in each **Cold Call** episode; keep the annotated WalkThru steps on the teacher's desk as a reminder.

The method must be quick to use and easy to integrate. The act of tracking sharpens awareness and provides immediate feedback.

4

REFLECT

After the lesson, the teacher can analyse what they noticed. You're not asking them to judge. This might typically happen alone, but great if you can get alongside them! Use prompts such as:

- Did I do what I planned?
- Where did it work well/where did it drift?
- What did I see from the students?

Help the teacher to make sense of it, not just crunch data. Try to connect to specific moments, student responses or environmental cues. This strengthens metacognitive control and deepens their reasoning.

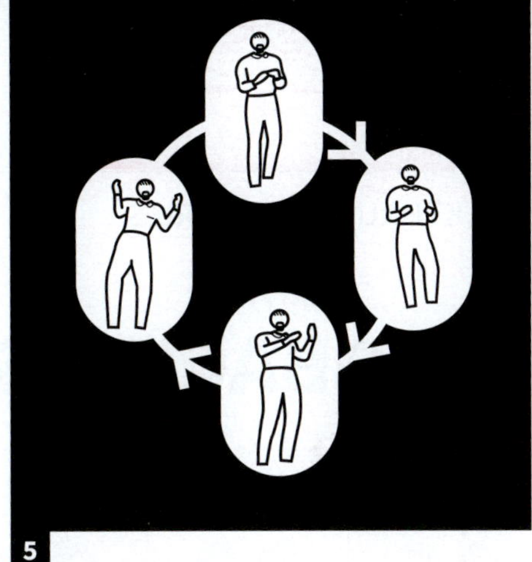

5

RESPOND

This process should ideally only lead to one small adjustment at a time. It's fine-tuning — changing the wording, refining the prompt, shifting the timing or using a new cue. The aim is for the teacher to identify and act on one practical refinement for the next lesson.

Over time, this repeated cycle builds fluency and control, supporting the shift towards intentional practice.

FEEDBACK & SUPPORT

Coaching conversations are pivotal moments where coaches and teachers come together to make sense of what is happening in the classroom and plan next steps. The WalkThrus in this collection offer practical tools for managing dialogue, structuring conversations and staying close to the core teaching focus. At the centre is The 5Ps Framework, which helps coaches guide purposeful conversations, whether one-to-one or in teams, by affirming progress, surfacing difficulties and identifying next steps.

THE DYNAMICS OF DIALOGUE

Coaching conversations should balance the importance of co-constructing feedback and actions with the need to be productive and action-focused. The dynamics are key, yet this is something that coaches often find difficult. Some conversations drift, others become too heavily coach-led. The best coaching dialogue sits in the middle — purposeful, responsive and grounded in teacher thinking. This WalkThru explores the ebb and flow of effective coaching dialogue — how to listen, respond and move the conversation forward.

1

RESPECT EXPERTISE

Coaching only works when it respects teacher expertise. If you start by telling, not listening, nothing sticks. Let the teacher go first.

Find out about their class and their intentions for the lesson. Ask what they saw, what they think, what they'd do next. Don't waste time stating the obvious — focus on what they don't yet see.

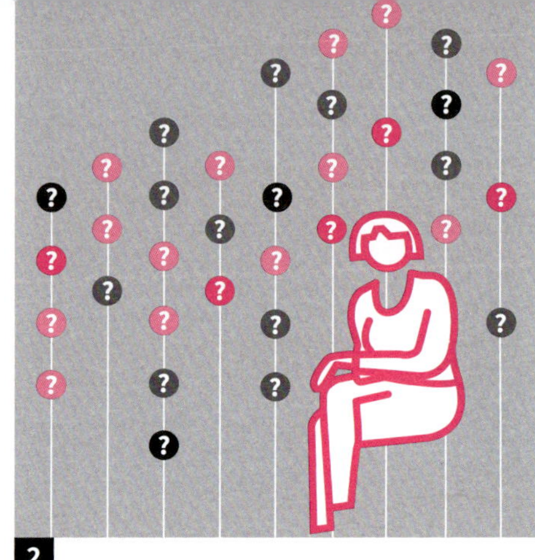

2

ASK QUESTIONS

Bring shape and purpose to the conversation, and prompt deep thinking from the teacher, by using questions. Use **Questions to Build Clarity** to explore thinking, intentions and decision-making, then use **Questions to Build Insight** to support sense-making. Use **Questions to Build Action** to determine what to do next.

3

ALLOW THE TEACHER TO EXPLORE THEIR THINKING

Once you ask a question, step back. Let the teacher talk first — about their intentions, what worked and what didn't. They need to think hard about what to change and why.

Give them space to try to make sense of what they noticed in the classroom. In groups, pair teachers up so everyone gets time to talk. Thinking comes before action.

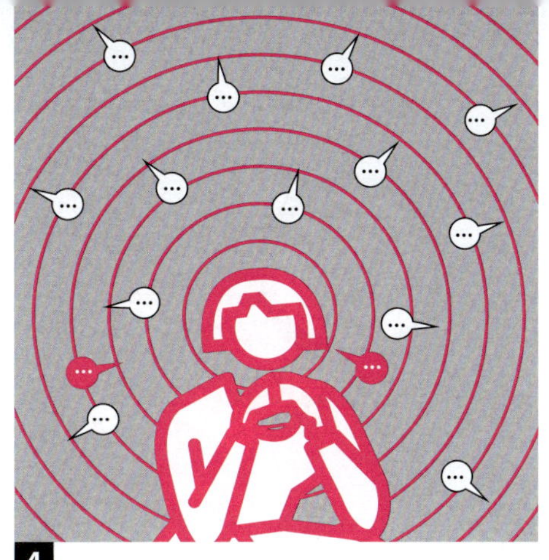

4

LISTEN & RESPOND

Use the steps in **Listening** to really get a sense of the teacher's perspective. Pick up on key ideas, probe deeper and clarify thinking.

Offer your own insights when needed — this can be sensitive, so the guidance in **Sharing Insights** can help. Coaching isn't about withholding expertise — it's about using it at the right time.

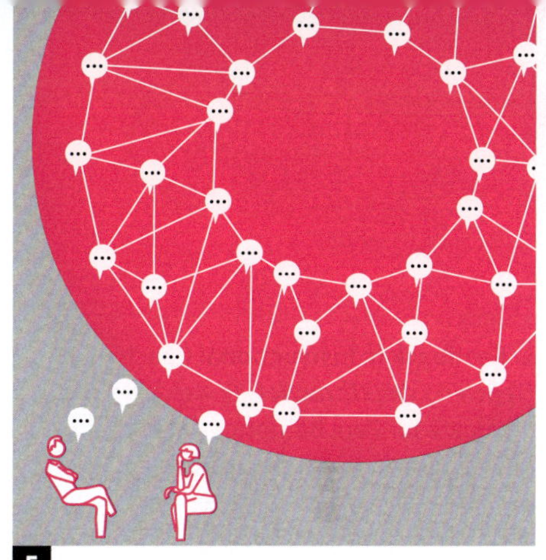

5

MORE DEPTH, LESS HASTE

Remember that coaching dialogue isn't a one-off event. Each conversation fits into a bigger cycle of improvement. Take time to get the details right.

Don't rush to the next step — work on what matters now, so progress is deliberate and lasting.

THE 5Ps FRAMEWORK

In **Feedback In Instructional Coaching** (*Teaching WalkThrus Vol. 2*), we advocate for Paul Bambrick Santoyo's 5Ps approach. It's useful to have an overarching framework to keep dialogue purposeful. But it's important to remember that this framework isn't often the agenda for our conversations, more a mechanism to help us organise the teacher's thinking. The 5Ps are best used as a tool for co-constructing feedback (see **Co-construction | Build it, don't send it**).

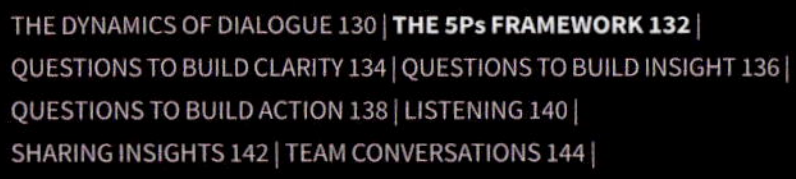

1

PRECISE PRAISE

Avoid the temptation to award praise in the sense that you are impressed or you like what you've seen. There's a risk that this will lead to a culture of approval-seeking. Instead, use **Questions to Build Clarity** and **Questions to Build Insight** to affirm the specific elements of the lesson, technique or step that have landed successfully in the classroom.

This is a co-constructed process; the teacher and coach stamping in the specific features that have worked well.

2

PROBE

Move through the coaching dialogue, aiming to uncover the elements of the lesson, technique or step that haven't yet landed successfully in the classroom. **Questions to Build Insight** help to surface these areas so that you can examine them properly alongside the teacher.

Again, this is a co-constructed process: don't let it become a litany of things that you didn't like. Instead, see it as a shared endeavour to make visible the important things that need attention.

3

PROBLEM & ACTION STEP

This part of the framework relies on both the teacher and the coach sharing a commitment to a breakthrough. The default disposition is always that habit change is hard and even the most effective, confident teachers will have problems to address.

Use **Questions to Build Action** to work out what those problems are and determine the steps the teacher will need to take.

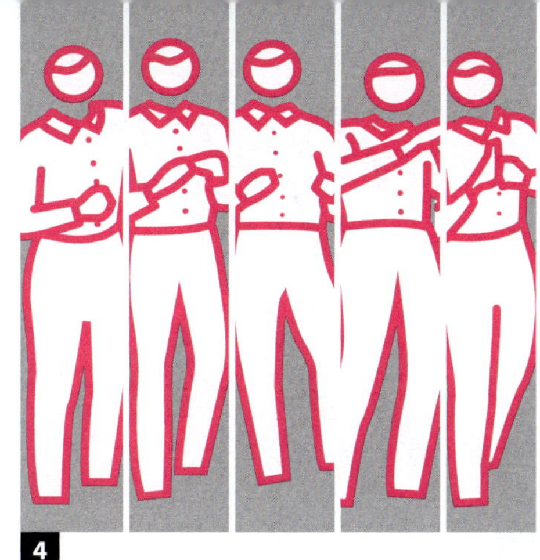

4

PRACTISE

This is an important test in your ability to be agile as a coach. As each new problem is uncovered, you're considering whether this is the sticking point — the thing that needs to be addressed right now. This means that you need to change modes as a coach. A new action step is created and it needs to be workshopped — modelled, **A|D|A|P|T**-ed and rehearsed — there and then. The WalkThrus in **Train & Model** will help, but it's crucial to secure a shared understanding of what that action step will look like in practice.

5

PLAN

We need to plan actively for improvement to happen. Action steps need to be recorded for future reference so we can be very intentional and later ask, 'Did you do the things you said you were going to do?'

The final step in the coaching conversation is to agree a timescale appropriate to the issue in hand, ideally in days and weeks, not months. Bambrick-Santoyo describes processes where teachers and their coaches have lots of very light, lean, short interactions rather than a few heavy-duty interactions.

QUESTIONS TO BUILD CLARITY

When you watch a lesson or a video of a teacher at work, you're only seeing a snapshot of their reality. It's not enough to make firm decisions or draw conclusions about what's working, what isn't or why.

Start coaching conversations with **Questions to Build Clarity.** Use them early to establish the learning context, understand the teacher's intentions and explore the thinking behind their actions. It's important not to bring assumptions to the conversation. Instead, ask questions that help to build a shared starting point.

1

SITUATION QUESTIONS

Establish the context for learning — what has come before this point, what the class has done well or struggled with, and what the learning culture of the class is. This means that you can better understand what is happening now. Use situation questions to build a clear understanding of the teaching and learning context before diving into specifics. For example, ask:

- *Can you tell me a little bit about your class?*
- *What have they been learning about, and how have they been getting on?*
- *What kind of things have you been working on in your own practice?*

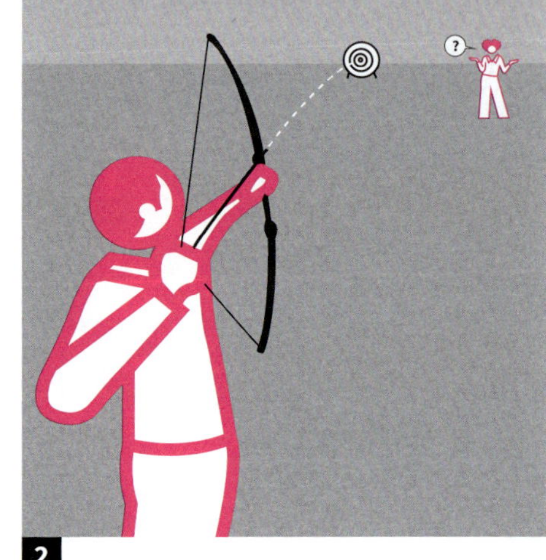

2

GOAL QUESTIONS

Clarify the teacher's intentions for the lesson, what they wanted students thinking about, talking about, doing and achieving, so that you can focus on the purpose behind their instructional choices. Use goal questions to establish a clear understanding of the teacher's intentions before you explore their classroom reality. For example, ask:

- *What was on your mind when you designed this lesson/selected this technique?*
- *What did you want students to know, understand or be able to do by the end?*
- *How does this connect to your longer-term goals for the class or your own practice?*

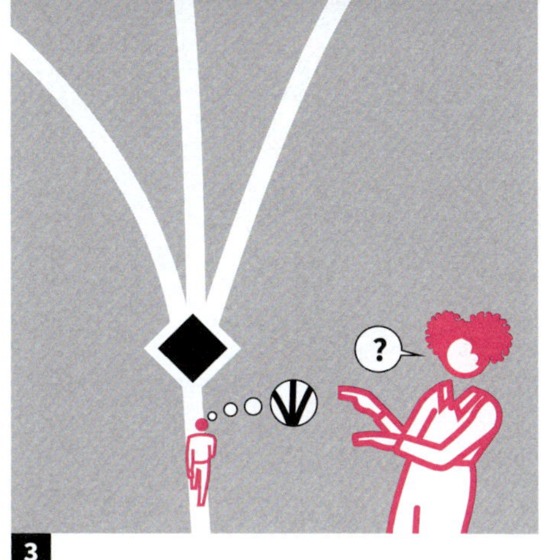

3

DECISION-MAKING QUESTIONS

Surface the reasoning behind instructional decisions. Working out what influenced the teacher's choices and what decision-drivers were at play helps you to understand the thought process driving the lesson. Use decision-making questions to uncover the rationale behind key teaching moves before evaluating their impact. For example, ask:

- *What drivers influenced your decision to use this approach at this time?*
- *What other options did you consider, and why did you choose this one?*
- *Did anything unexpected emerge that caused you to adjust your decision-making during the lesson?*

4

ACTION QUESTIONS

Examine what the teacher did in practice. How did they enact their decisions? Why did they do what they did? This prompts them to reflect on how their decision-drivers translated into concrete actions. Use action questions to clarify the specific steps taken and their intended impact. For example, ask:

- *How did your decision-drivers shape the actions you took during the lesson?*
- *What steps did you take to intentionally create the conditions where all students could…?*
- *How did you adapt your approach in response to what you noticed happening?*

5

PERCEPTION QUESTIONS

Understanding the extent to which all students are succeeding — what they understand, how deeply they are thinking, where they are struggling or how they can improve — is a key part of the cognitive coaching domain (see **Meaningful Coaching**). For example, ask:

- *What are you seeing from your students that gives you confidence that this approach is starting to land well?*
- *How do you think students got on here? Why do you think that?*
- *To what extent do you think that all students took what they needed from this moment?*

QUESTIONS TO BUILD INSIGHT

Once you've established what happened in the lesson, the next step is to explore why. It's not enough to simply replay events; you need to help the teacher make sense of them. Without deeper analysis, gaps between intention and reality can remain hidden, and opportunities to improve and refine get missed.

Use the questions in this WalkThru to highlight key moments, examine student responses and explore the impact of teaching decisions.

1

NOTICING QUESTIONS

Use noticing questions to examine what the teacher has spotted at key points in the lesson. This helps to build situation awareness and focus their attention on important moments that might otherwise be overlooked. For example, ask:

- *Did you notice any students that were finding the work difficult? What did you see?*
- *What did you notice about the students' attention levels here?*
- *What stood out to you about the way students responded to your questions? What did you notice about their responses?*

2

SCALING QUESTIONS

Help the teacher see if a gap exists between their intentions for the lesson and the classroom reality. Use scaling questions carefully as they can feel judgemental. Scale against specific moments. For example, ask:

- *On a scale of 1-10, how successful were students in enacting your intentions?*
- *What did you see from students that pleased you here?*
- *What might you like to have seen that isn't quite there yet?*

The aim isn't to agree or disagree. It's to open a space between intention and reality.

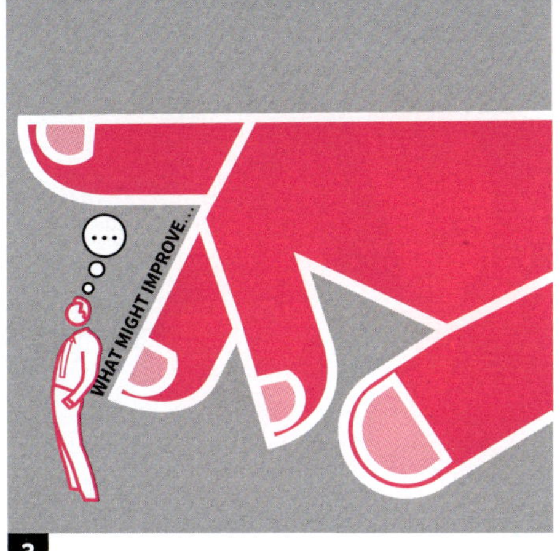

3

NUDGE QUESTIONS

If you've used a scaling question to establish a starting point, follow up with a series of nudge questions to help the teacher identify what student success might look like further up the scale. Small, sharp nudges can make improvements feel manageable. Nudges around quality, quantity and frequency work well. For example, ask:

- *What might improve the quality of the students' work? What's missing?*
- *How might you get more students involved? What might that look like?*
- *How could that happen more/less often?*

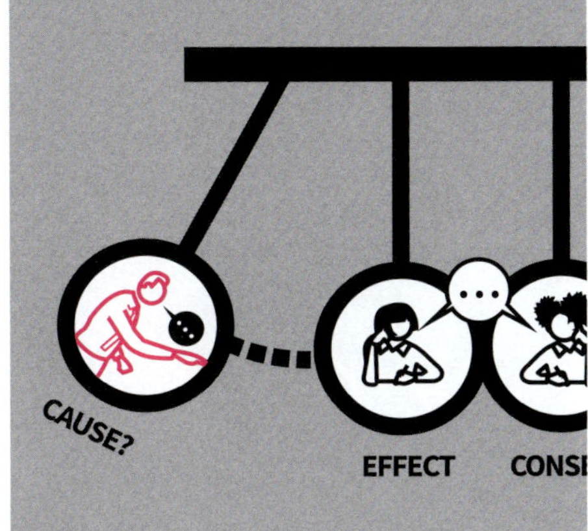

4

CAUSE & EFFECT QUESTIONS

Understanding why something happened helps to build the teacher's understanding and awareness of the classroom. Use cause & effect questions to help teachers connect what they've seen to underlying factors rather than relying on surface-level observations. For example, ask:

- Why do you think students responded in that way?
- What do you think caused them to struggle?
- What might they have been missing?
- What might be going on for the students here?

5

COUNTERFACTUAL QUESTIONS

Use counterfactual questions to help teachers to think about alternative scenarios, focusing in on the impact of their decisions and actions. In effect, you're helping them to design a more desirable outcome for students next time. For example, ask:

- *How do you think students would have responded if they'd had a little more thinking time?*
- *What if you had checked for understanding in a different way — how might that have changed the outcome?*
- *What might happen if that explanation was framed differently?*

QUESTIONS TO BUILD ACTION

Insight without action doesn't lead to change. Once teachers understand what's happening and why, the next step is to decide what to do about it. Without focus and clarity, coaching can drift into vague ideas and missed opportunities.

Use **Questions to Build Action** to bridge the gap between analysis and implementation. Help the teacher zoom in on what matters most, explore practical options and commit to clear next steps. These questions turn reflection into action, and action into real change in the classroom.

1

FOCUS QUESTIONS

Don't allow teachers to leave a coaching session with a long list of things to work on; it's likely that they might not know where to start. Try to define a singular, useful focus to ensure that their effort is directed to where it will matter most. For example, ask:

- *What might make the biggest difference now?*
- *Which of those changes do you think you need to tackle first? Why?*
- *What might be the most sensible starting point here?*

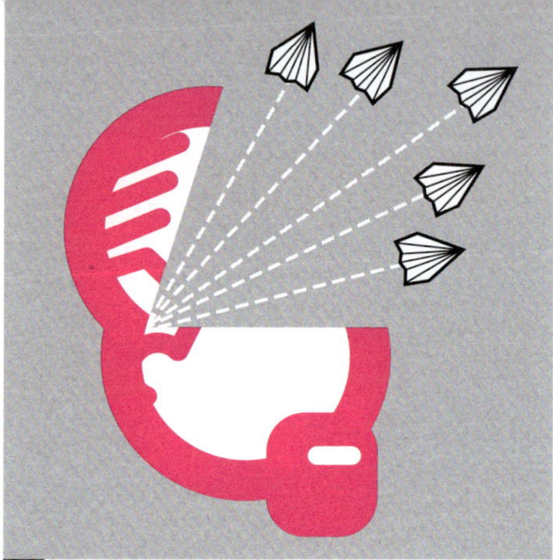

2

OPTION QUESTIONS

Generate options that will help the teacher to fulfil the action step. Explore multiple potential solutions, testing them out from different angles to assess their validity and usefulness. Use **Sharing Insights** if the teacher is struggling for ideas. For example, ask:

- *What could you do to make this happen?*
- *Why might that work?*
- *When wouldn't this technique work? Why not?*
- *Have you seen or tried any strategies that worked for you in a similar situation?*

3

SOLUTION QUESTIONS

Use the menu of options generated to identify a specific set of steps that will turn ideas into actionable solutions. Specificity is key — help the teacher to define precisely what they will do and how. For example, ask:

- *What will you do next?*
- *What does this look like tomorrow?*
- *What's your plan for putting this into practice?*

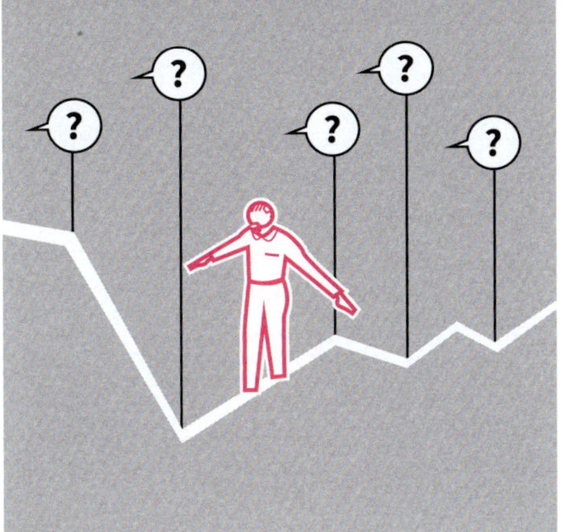

4

CHANGE QUESTIONS

Every teacher, almost without exception, wants the best for their students and therefore wants their teaching to be as effective as possible. Help the teachers to see that investing in the action steps will make things better for themselves and their students. Create a meaningful compulsion to act. Ask:

- *If we nailed this step, what difference would it make to your students?*
- *What difference would it make to you?*

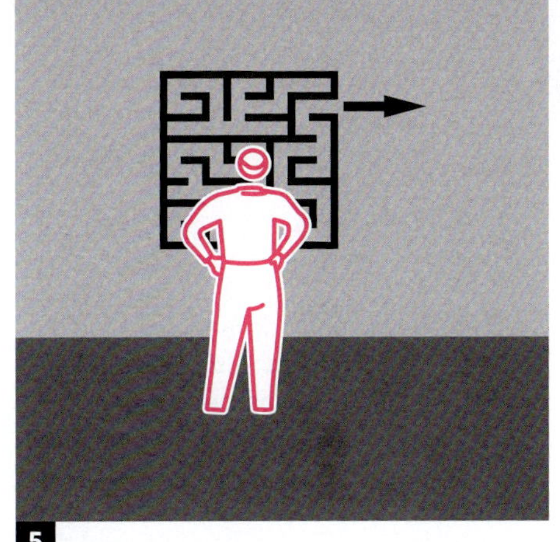

5

NEEDS QUESTIONS

Identify what is needed for success — including potential obstacles — to help teachers plan proactively and avoid roadblocks. Be honest about the barriers that might make implementation tricky, and plan to overcome them. For example, ask:

- *What support, resources or adjustments do you need to make this happen?*
- *Why might this not happen? What could get in the way?*
- *What could help make this change easier to sustain over time?*

LISTENING

As coaches, it's natural to want to offer solutions and ideas. But before we do that, we have to properly understand the challenges the teacher is facing. Skilful listening is the coach's superpower — it creates the space for real dialogue, prompts deeper thinking, brings clarity and builds trust. This isn't just about staying quiet; it's about being fully present, noticing what's said and what's not, and responding in ways that help the teacher organise, refine and extend their thinking. This WalkThru explores what that looks like in practice

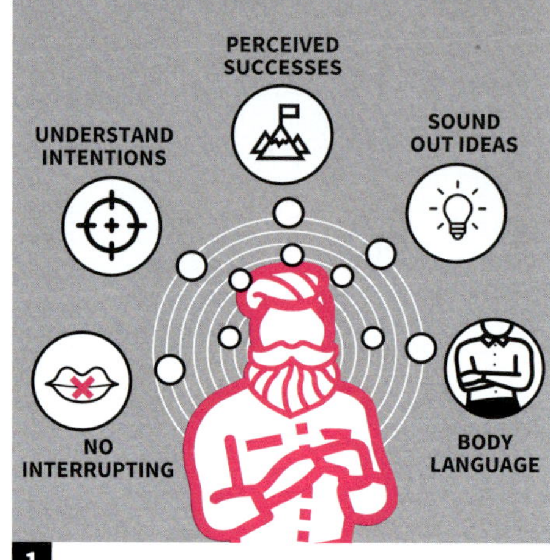

1

STEP BACK

Listen to the teachers' reflections without interrupting. Try to understand their intentions, and what they percieve to have been successful or not. Often, teachers need an opportunity to sound out their ideas — let them do this. Pay attention not only to what they are saying, but also to their body language and tone.

2

USE SILENCE TO SUPPORT THINKING

Give silent thinking time to allow teachers to formulate and articulate their ideas. Thinking is harder if we feel rushed, so create time and space for self-reflection. Silence not only communicates respect, but also usually leads to a more thorough response.

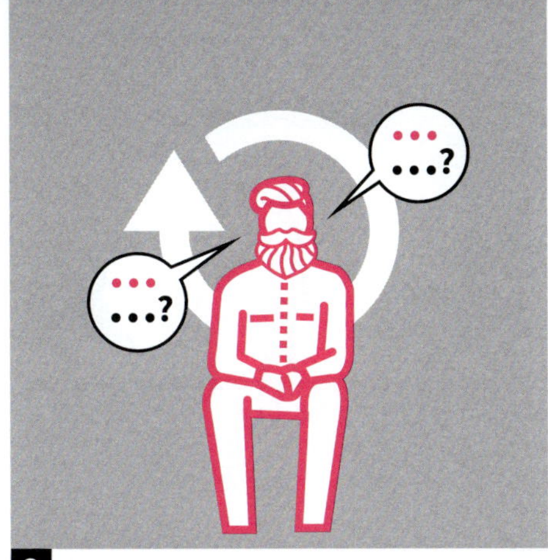

3

REPEAT BACK

When teachers' reflections are raw, they can sometimes lack cohesion. Repeat back important ideas to help them organise and refine their thinking:

- *... so you've mentioned three things there... X, Y and Z — is that right?*
- *... let's go back to the things that really pleased you here — you said that...*

4

PARAPHRASE

As you listen, prepare yourself to paraphrase what you have heard. Instead of just repeating back, summarise the teachers' ideas to show them that you have listened and to check your understanding. You can't do this everytime, so seek out key moments inbetween conversation phases or questioning sequences.

5

CLARIFY MEANING

Routinely clarify what you have heard, aiming for specificity and precision. Prompt the teacher to explore the rationale for their thinking:

- *... and what did you see from the students that made you think that?*
- *... when you say students, did you mean all students or some students? How many?*
- *... you said that you were unhappy with their responses — what do you think was missing?*

SHARING INSIGHTS

Coaches sometimes hesitate to share their own knowledge, worried it might make the process feel top-down or overly directive. But there's a difference between imposing opinions and offering valuable insights.

Coaching isn't about withholding expertise — it's about knowing when and how to share it. If a coach has useful knowledge that could help a teacher, they should offer it at the right moment, ensuring it supports thinking rather than replaces it.

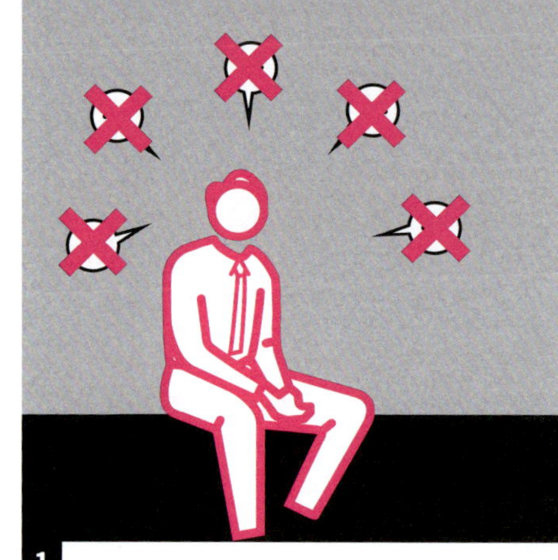

1

TAME YOUR ADVICE MONSTER

Hold back from giving advice too quickly. In *The Coaching Habit*, Bungay Stanier calls this the Advice Monster — the impulse to jump in with solutions before a teacher has had the chance to think for themselves. The issue isn't giving advice; it's making advice your default response.

MICHAEL BUNGAY STANIER

Tell less and ask more.
Your advice is not as good
As you think it is.

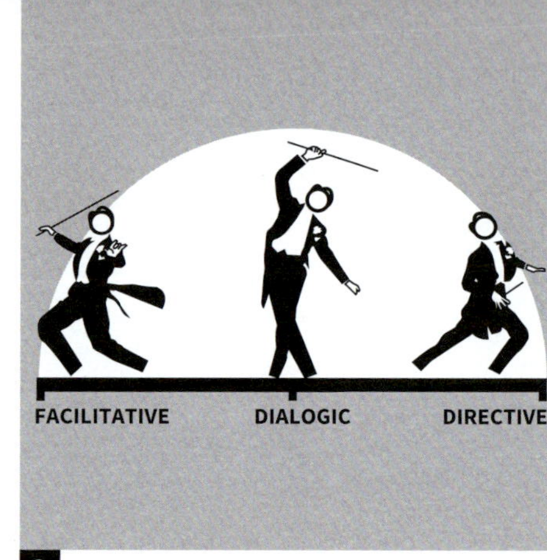

2

FLEX ALONG THE COACHING CONTINUUM

Jim Knight's coaching continuum places facilitative coaching at one end and directive coaching at the other, with dialogical coaching in the centre.

Imagine yourself tethered to this middle ground — you can flex in either direction, but always have the sense that you're being pulled back to the centre. Lean more towards facilitative when a teacher needs space to think, or more directive when they need a little bit of what you have to offer.

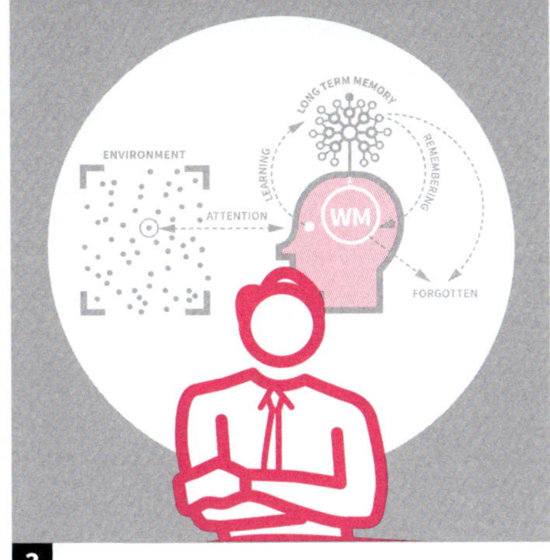

3

DON'T WITHHOLD EXPERTISE

This doesn't mean defaulting to advice-giving, but it does mean that the work must be informed by a deep understanding of how learning happens and strong knowledge of effective teaching techniques. When the time is right, offer insights that help the teacher build a shared understanding of the problem and its possible solutions. Holding back when expertise is needed doesn't serve the teacher or their students.

4

OFFER, DON'T IMPOSE

As in **The Dynamics of Dialogue**, let the teacher explore their thinking first. Then, if you have useful ideas to share, offer them tentatively:

- *Would you mind if I shared some ideas about that?*
- *Would it be OK if I suggested something here?*
- *Can I tell you what I noticed at that point?*

Remember, a dialogue is a two-way exchange; it's not a dialogue if you withhold knowledge that might be useful.

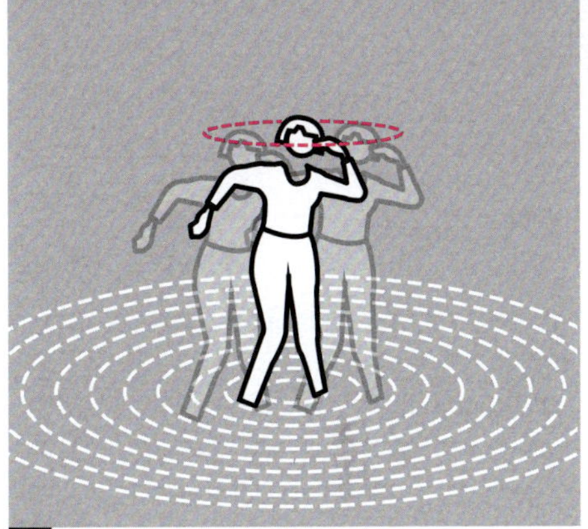

5

PEOPLE DON'T KNOW WHAT THEY DON'T KNOW

Don't leave the teacher guessing at something that they might not know yet. People can only think about what they know so there's little sense in trying to tease out knowledge that doesn't exist. Be useful, ready to bring to the conversation things that might otherwise be missing:

- What you noticed in the classroom.
- Student engagement and achievement data.
- Reliable knowledge about cognition and learning.
- Teaching techniques that you can describe and model effectively.

TEAM CONVERSATIONS

Our fieldwork has demonstrated that the 5Ps feedback process devised by Paul Bambrick-Santoyo applies to team coaching as well as to coaching individuals. Once established, the protocol informs observations and subsequent team feedback.

The team leader can use the 5Ps to guide the conversation in a systematic manner, taking care to structure each meeting so that every individual contributes. Individual goals can be established, aligning strongly with the overarching team goals. After some intial modelling, leaders should let their team members lead each discussion.

1

PRECISE PRAISE: EXCHANGE SUCCESSES

Start by exploring examples of where the techniques under discussion have been effective, with teachers taking the lead. Model precision and focus in the responses, supported by the WalkThrus visuals, step by step, to focus discussions. In pairs, teachers can share examples and then the team leader can offer more, based on their last round of observations. Affirming success and progress reinforces habits and is a powerful motivator. **Dynamics of Dialogue** is a helpful guide.

2

PROBE: ESTABLISH COMMON CHALLENGES

Let's Probe! Before leaders offer their own feedback, it's helpful to form pairs to explore any challenges experienced enacting the agreed action steps. In pairs, teachers can open up and share genuine problems they've experienced. These issues are then shared with the whole team.

Leaders might then reinforce the teachers' evaluations and contribute their own views based on their observations. Probing is about surfacing problems, not about judgement.

3

PROBLEM: AGREE COMMON FOCUS AREAS

After surfacing some of the common challenges, the discussion should shift to identifying the most important areas to work on over the next cycle.

Here each individual teacher might select their own focus area, based on the probe discussion, or it might be better for everyone to align and work on the same thing. Leader-coaches can guide this based on their overall sense of the key priorities.

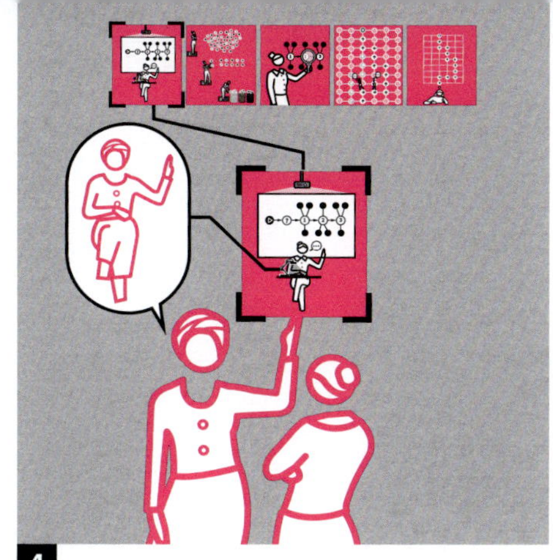

4

PRACTISE: EXPLORE & REHEARSE NEXT STEPS

As always, it's vital to explore the mental model each teacher has formed regarding the ideas and actions discussed. It's a mistake to assume everyone has understood and will then enact techniques in the same agreed way.

It's helpful to use pairs again to check for understanding, each teacher running through how they will apply the technique with more precision in their context. In some cases, it's possible to rehearse scripts or to practise a technique in the meeting.

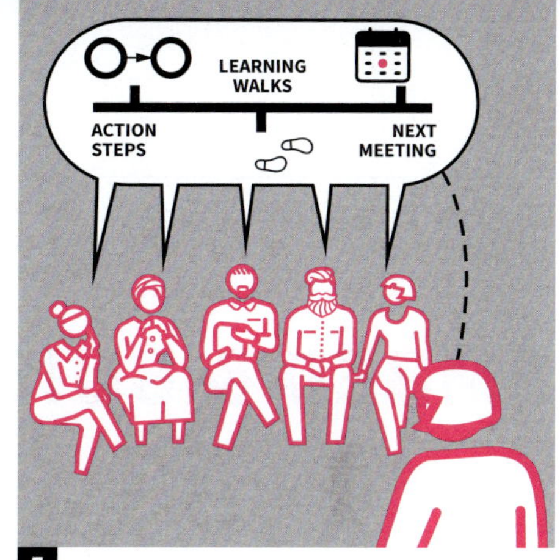

5

PLAN: AGREE THE TIMESCALE FOR PRACTICE & OBSERVATION

Meetings should conclude with detailed planning of subsequent actions:

- Which action steps will be focused on.
- When any learning walks or paired observations will happen, taking any lesson cover needs into account.
- When the next meeting is — confirm the overall timeframe, establishing a sense of immediacy about the practice in lessons.

This process then forms a loop, repeated from session to session.

WALKTHRU **WHAT?** SERIES

EMBED & BUILD

Embedding a new technique takes time, support and sustained focus. The Embed & Build series provides practical ways to help teachers embed new techniques over time. These WalkThrus focus on habits, consolidation and sustained improvement. Coaches will find tools for using prompts, cues and checklists, alongside guidance on recognising key stages of learning and supporting teachers to build fluency. This section also revisits our Clustering concept, designed to help teachers connect and extend their practice by building on what's working.

PROMPTS, CUES & CHECKLISTS

Research findings from the EEF (2021) highlight the importance of providing prompts and cues that nudge teachers to consistently apply new techniques. At the back end of a coaching cycle, these prompts help to consolidate new teaching habits and prevent them from drifting. With the demands of daily teaching, it's easy for new methods to lose momentum.

The five steps outlined here provide practical strategies to keep these techniques front and centre.

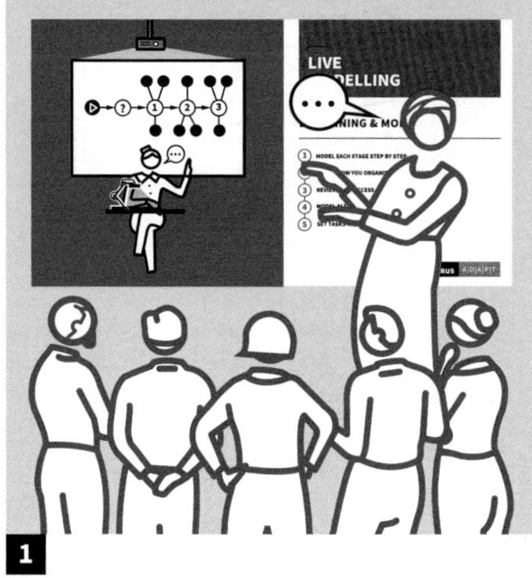

1

KEEP IT FRONT & CENTRE

Curate a culture where great teaching and learning is on everyone's mind, all of the time. Ensure new ideas remain visible and are consistently reinforced. Talk about them in every staff briefing and team meeting. Model core techniques by using them in assemblies, in the lunch line and in your daily interactions. Be seen doing them — to remind everyone that they're part of the fabric of school life.

Avoid the temptation to build WalkThru hexagon displays — they're never a substitute for the technique actually happening in the classroom.

2

USE INDIVIDUALISED CLASSROOM PROMPTS

Co-create clear, simple prompts that help the teacher use the new technique precisely in their classroom. These might be visual reminders focusing on a whole technique or specific steps:

- An annotated WalkThru on the teacher's desk.
- An A3 page at the back of the room reminding the teacher to give thinking time during **Cold Call** or **Think, Pair, Share.**

The key is to work with teachers to design prompts that are useful to them, offering explicit reminders for difficult habit changes, rather than imposing them.

3

SPECIFY & REHEARSE SITUATION-SPECIFIC CUES

Work with the teacher to identify the first domino — a natural cue that occurs during a lesson. Specify the actions the teacher will take when this cue arises. For example:

- A partially correct answer as the cue for **Say It Again Better.**
- An 'I don't know' response as the cue for **No Opt Out.**

Practise these responses until they become automatic. This could involve **Training Room Rehearsal** or **Classroom Rehearsal.** The goal is for teachers to apply strategies independently, responding to cues as they naturally arise in the classroom.

4

USE CHECKLISTS

Use checklists to emphasise the key ingredients of a new technique. This is even more concise than the five-step format of a WalkThru — it's the core mechanisms that enable the technique to function — e.g. **Think, Pair, Share** might include:

- Ask an important, open question.
- Check that everyone has a partner.
- Give individual thinking time.
- Circulate without getting caught up in individual conversations.

Encourage teachers to use checklists regularly, adjusting as they become more confident with the technique.

5

LEAN INTO TEAMS

Team structures offer a naturally supportive environment to consolidate new techniques. Run regular meetings that focus on specific aspects of the technique, using prompts, cues and shared checklists to maintain momentum.

Encourage informal conversations in corridors and classrooms to reinforce the focus. Help teams find the common ground that often exists when teachers are working with shared approaches within a common curriculum.

SUPPORTING CONSOLIDATION

It's not enough for a teacher to use a technique once; it must become second nature — the choice they make even when no one is watching. This requires ongoing, practical support to ensure techniques are fully embedded.

A well-planned coaching cycle is crucial, but coaches and leaders must be prepared to provide that extra push to help teachers stamp in changes properly and create the conditions where good practice is amplified across the school.

1

KEEP GIVING FEEDBACK

Progress can stall when teachers stop receiving useful feedback. Ongoing feedback is key to helping them stay focused on consolidating new techniques, especially towards the end of a coaching cycle.

This might mean that you need to look for informal feedback opportunities — drop-ins, casual chats or quick check-ins before or after lessons. Be proactive and make yourself available for quick tweaks. This ongoing support helps the teacher make important final adjustments before the technique becomes fully embedded.

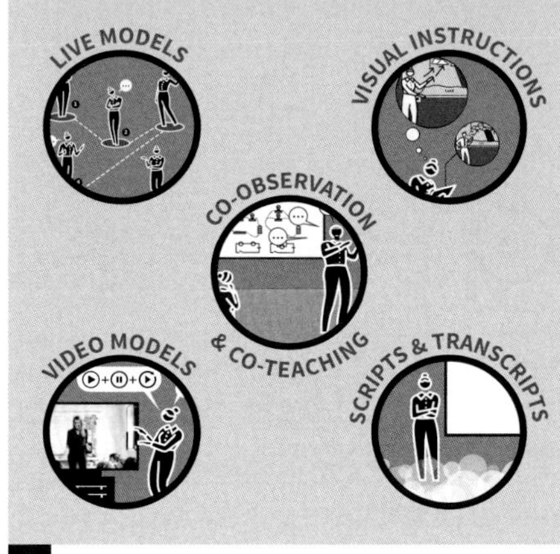

2

PROVIDE ADDITIONAL MODELS

Teachers often adapt techniques over time, but this can lead to drift, where techniques unintentionally change. At this stage, additional models help teachers stay on track and continue to refine their practice. Even late in the cycle, provide examples — live models, video examples or transcripts.

Use the **Ways of Modelling** guidance to offer clear, specific examples for comparison. This helps teachers adjust and keep their implementation aligned with the technique's intended purpose.

3

BUILD A RESOURCE LIBRARY

Create a digital resource library accessible to teachers whenever they need it. Fill it with videos, scripts, articles, checklists and other materials that support specific techniques. Encourage teachers, coaches and leaders to contribute and share what's working in their classrooms. This library becomes a powerful, evolving resource for your PD system, with real-world examples of techniques in action. For example, video clips of teachers or leaders modelling techniques can be especially useful in helping others see how it's done.

4

USE VIDEO

Teachers can stamp in a technique by using video self-observation. As we've explored elsewhere in this book, video is a powerful tool but must remain low stakes, with teachers choosing to record key moments in their lessons to reflect on privately. At the end of the coaching cycle, video helps teachers assess how well the technique is landing with students and identify areas for adjustment.

While coaches can guide this process (see **Using Video**), the key is making video a personal tool for ongoing improvement.

5

PEER COLLABORATION

After coaching cycles, create opportunities for teachers to collaborate and share their work. Use team meetings to discuss progress, challenges and classroom impact. Organise regular, structured sessions for teachers to meet, review what's working and plan next steps or improvements.

Form PLCs where teachers focusing on similar techniques build expert hubs. Even show-and-tell sessions during staff training days can be effective. The aim is to turn teachers into support mechanisms for each other, supporting consolidation and amplifying impact across the school.

HABIT STACKING

In *Atomic Habits* (2018), James Clear recommends habit stacking to build strong routines by linking smaller actions together. In coaching, this means helping teachers blend techniques naturally rather than using them in isolation. Support teachers in using this approach to embed new habits and build their practice over time.

One of the best ways to build a new habit is to identify a current habit you already do each day and then stack your new behavior on top.

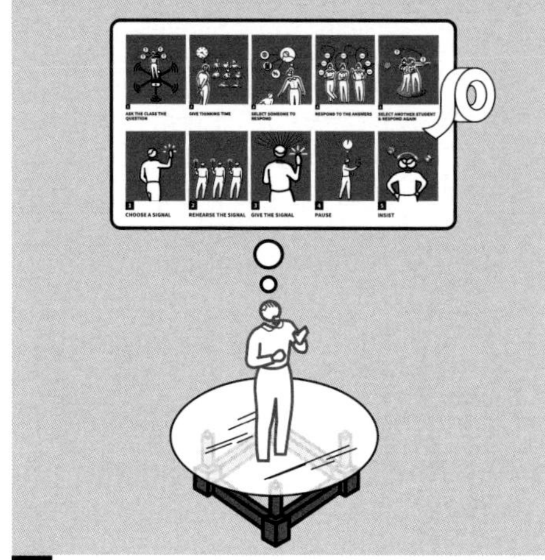

1 START WITH AN EMBEDDED TECHNIQUE

Identify a technique that the teacher already uses regularly, intentionally and with little conscious effort. This habit will act as the foundation for building a new routine. New habits are easier to implement when linked to something the teacher already does automatically. By starting with a familiar technique, you reduce cognitive load and increase the chances of the new technique sticking.

If the teacher already uses **Signal, Pause, Insist** effectively, use this as the base for layering a new technique, such as **Cold Calling**.

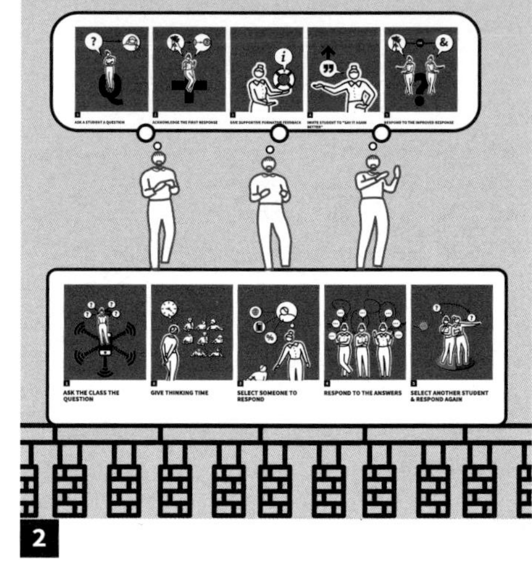

2 MAKE THE CONNECTION OBVIOUS

The new technique should feel like a logical extension of the existing one, reinforcing its purpose. The connection between the two must feel natural, rather than a forced add-on. If the connection isn't obvious, it's less likely the teacher will remember to implement the new technique consistently.

If **Cold Calling** is embedded and all students are participating, the next step might be **Say It Again Better** to improve response quality. This supports **Cold Calling** by helping students express their ideas more clearly.

3

ATTACH THE NEW TECHNIQUE

Help the teacher create a link between the existing routine and the new technique using the habit stacking formula: 'After [current habit], I will use [new habit].' This makes the new habit an automatic extension of the first. By linking the two techniques, you make it easier for the teacher to apply both consistently. For example:

- 'After using a **Worked Example**, I will use **Show-Me Boards** to check for understanding.'

Now, the teacher's use of a **Worked Example** triggers the follow-up of checking for understanding with **Show-Me Boards**.

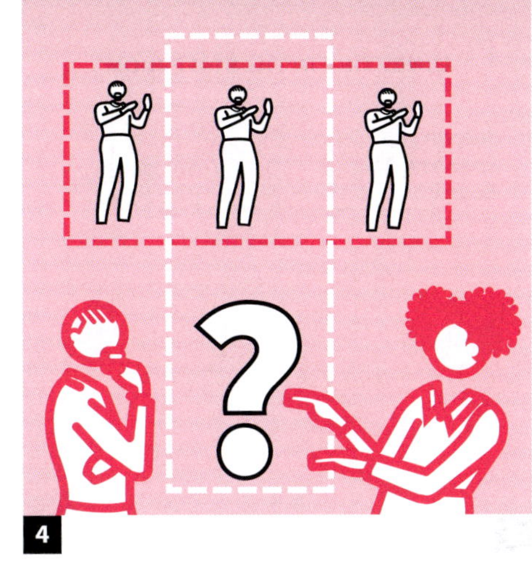

4

EXPAND THE STACK OVER TIME

Once the new habit is automatic, gradually add more techniques to the stack. Each new habit should build on what's already in place, increasing fluency and consistency. Layering habits over time allows the teacher to refine their practice without feeling overwhelmed. This iterative expansion ensures the new techniques become second nature and the teacher can use them more confidently in their classroom.

A teacher who has embedded **Signal, Pause, Insist** and **Cold Calling** can then add **Say It Again Better**, followed by **Think, Pair, Share**, creating a strong cluster for deepening student thinking.

5

STACK TOGETHER IN TEAMS

Apply habit stacking to curriculum or phase teams. Work with the team to identify shared routines and enhance them through habit stacking, ensuring all members embed the same core techniques for a cohesive approach.

When teams stack habits together, it strengthens the teaching culture and ensures consistency. It also fosters peer support, as teachers reinforce each other's practices.

STAGES OF LEARNING

Teachers don't implement new techniques overnight — and they rarely get it right the first time. Based on Jim Knight's research and practice, this WalkThru outlines five predictable stages teachers go through when adopting a new technique. It's important to recognise which stage the teacher is working at in order to best support them to fully embed the change. Sometimes a mechanical enactment is a good start, but proficiency is the goal. Moving on too quickly can lead to problems further down the line.

JIM KNIGHT

1

NON-USE

Teachers are not using the technique — either because they don't know about it, or they're resisting it. They may have missed a training workshop or lack clarity about what the technique looks like. Others may resist actively or passively.

Identify whether the barrier is awareness or resistance. If awareness is the issue, revisit the rationale and clearly model the technique. If resistance is present, surface concerns without judgement. Our steps in **Theory | The Cognitive Argument** might be helpful here.

2

AWARENESS

Teachers are aware of the technique but haven't tried it. They may be interested, even enthusiastic, but haven't yet taken the first step. Delay at this stage increases the risk of forgetting or losing motivation.

Support the teacher to choose a small, low-stakes context to try out the technique (e.g. one class, one question type, one phase of the lesson). Use **Do It | Training Room Rehearsal** to help them feel prepared — for instance, scripting a **Signal, Pause, Insist** prompt or practising an explanation out loud.

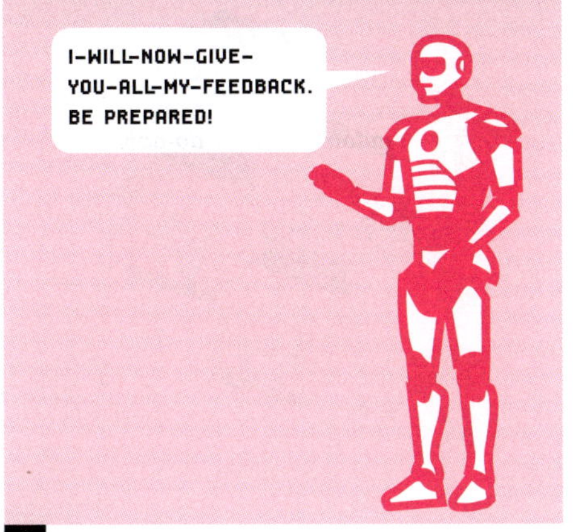

3

MECHANICAL

It's quite common to see teachers trying a technique, but it coming off as clunky or forced. This is the mental demand of juggling new habits and old routines. Think of a teacher awkwardly trying to embed **Cold Call**, stumbling over their phrasing or accepting called-out responses.

In reality, this is a sign that while they're heading in the right direction, they're not there yet. Give continued, focused feedback on small refinements, avoiding overwhelming them with too many changes at once.

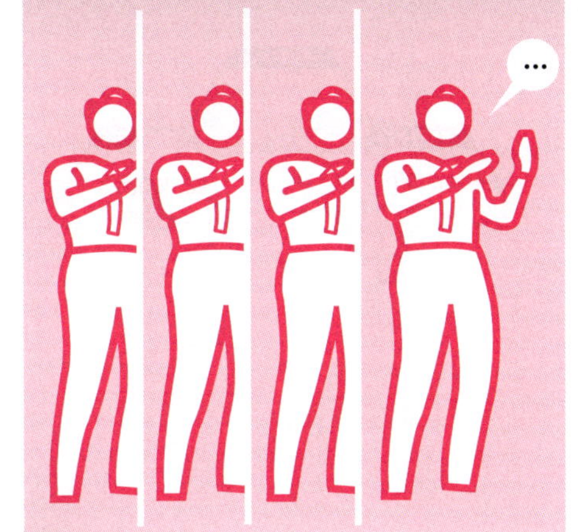

4

ROUTINE

Teachers are using the technique consistently — but in a fixed, habitual way. They're no longer struggling to remember it, but they may not quite be using it at the right time, for the right reason. This brings a risk of *false clarity* — assuming the technique is working well without checking its impact on learning.

Use **Questions to Build Insight** to encourage reflection and surface boundary conditions. Plan for intentional adjustments that deepen the technique's effectiveness.

5

PROFICIENT

This is ultimately the aim of our work — to support teachers to use techniques fluently and flexibly. For example, a proficient teacher using **Show-Me Boards** will run the routine precisely, at the right time, for the right purpose. They'll switch and adapt in the moment, interweaving **Cold Call** or **Think, Pair, Share** to explore student thinking further.

At this stage, support is less about fixing and more about sharpening. How can we stamp this in? How can we build on and connect this technique to other routines?

CLUSTERS & CONNECTED MOVES

At the end of a coaching cycle, clusters help you guide teachers in identifying their next steps by grouping related techniques that work together. Just like dance steps or writing techniques form a routine, techniques are most effective when sequenced and combined. Our digital **Cluster Tools** ensure continuity, helping to connect new techniques to what's already been worked on. Here are five ways to use clusters to drive next steps.

1

MOVE THROUGH YOUR COMMON-PRIORITY CLUSTER

A common approach in many schools is to identify a cluster of techniques as a shared focus. For example, if the goal is to improve basic learning behaviours, a cluster from **Behaviour & Relationships** can be selected. This approach is shaped by teacher discussions, ensuring everyone has input.

At the end of a coaching cycle, the next step is to move to the next technique in the cluster, continuing the focus and building on progress made.

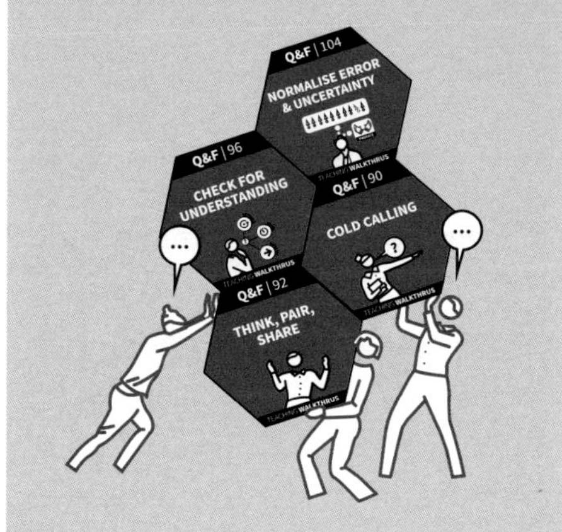

2

SOLVE THE NEXT PART OF THE PROBLEM

Some learning problems are too complex for a single technique. This is where our **Problem-Solution Cluster Tool** comes in, offering a cluster of potential solutions for common learning challenges. For example, to involve all students in questioning, **Cold Calling** is a good start.

But to fully address the issue, the teacher needs a broader range of techniques, such as **Think, Pair, Share** or **Show-Me Boards**, to ensure high participation. Use this approach to decide which technique to work on next.

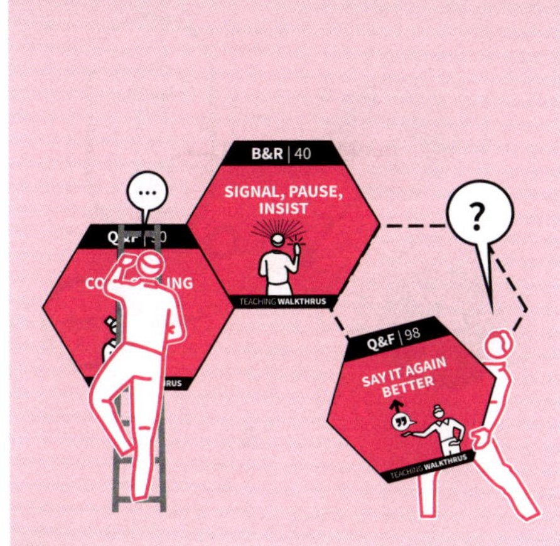

3

BUILD ON INITIAL SUCCESS

If a technique has been successfully implemented, clusters provide a way to build on that success. They can serve as **Mental Models**, combining techniques into a cohesive instructional script or connected move. For example, if **Signal, Pause, Insist** is working well, the teacher could introduce **Cold Call** to get all students thinking, followed by **Say It Again Better** to refine responses and deepen understanding.

Use these causal structures to help teachers work out where to go next.

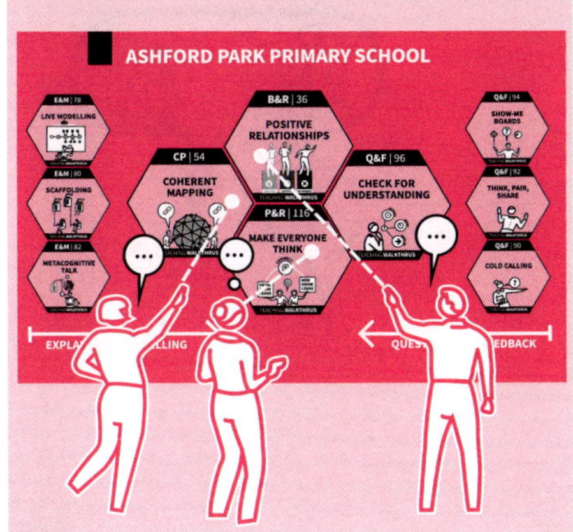

4

CONNECT TO TEAM OR SCHOOL PRIORITIES

When we talk about **Three-Stream CPD**, there's a cluster link, too. If a teacher is working on an individual technique, their next step might be to connect it to a team or whole-school priority.

When everyone aligns in this way, it becomes easier to align these three streams. This could involve identifying the link between individual work and the team focus. Alternatively, it could mean taking an individual next step that builds on a shared core across the team or school.

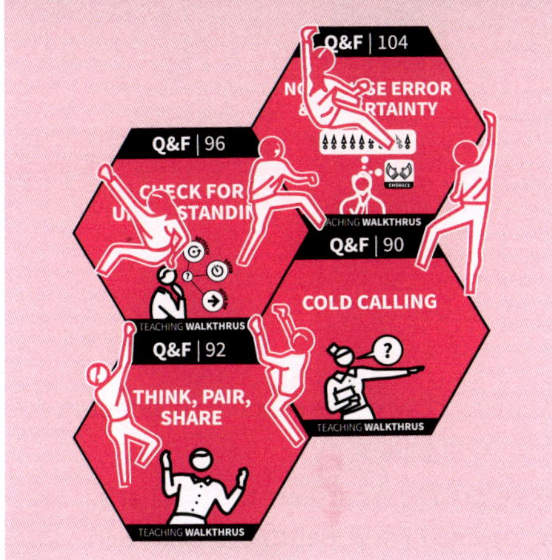

5

SOLVE THE NEXT LEARNING PROBLEM

At the end of a coaching cycle, the next step might be to solve the next learning problem. Revisit the steps in **Solving Learning Problems** to identify where students are struggling and select a cluster of potential solutions.

Zoom in on the most likely starting point and focus on the technique that will address the issue most effectively

TRIANGULATION | WHEN TO MOVE ON

The objective of the coaching dialogue is to triangulate:

INTENTION | What were the teacher's intentions? What was the goal? What did they expect/predict would be the outcome?

AWARENESS | The extent to which the teacher is aware of how successfully students are thinking, making meaning, practising and rehearsing.

REALITY | The extent to which the reality matches the intention — as coaches, we can provide insight here, too.

1

WHY | INTENTIONS & GOALS

Use coaching dialogue to explore the teacher's understanding of the technique. This will be clear in how well they can articulate its purpose and how it connects to their goals. If their understanding feels weak or unclear, it's a sign that more work is needed.

For example, if the goal is to increase thinking ratio using **Cold Calling**, ask the teacher how they believe this technique will help. Can they link the technique directly to the problem they want to solve? Is their application of the technique driven by a clear understanding of its purpose?

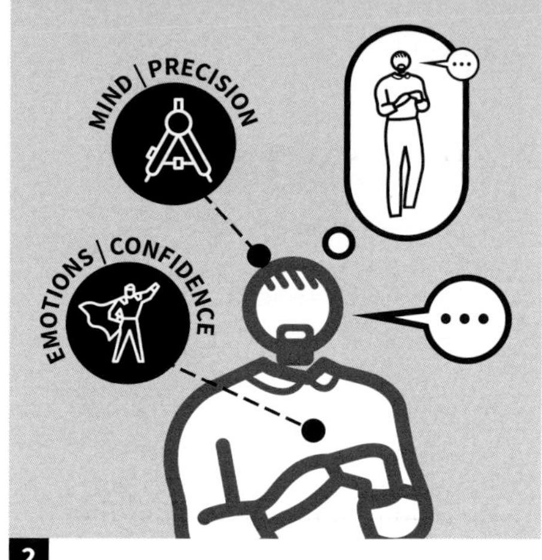

2

WHAT | TECHNIQUE & EXECUTION

The teacher should be able to use the technique with enough precision and confidence to meet the goal. Think about the business end in **Stages of Learning** — are they proficient? Are the steps clear and intentional, or has the technique drifted? If the teacher is adapting the technique to suit different needs, it's a sign of successful embedding.

For example, if the teacher is using **Think, Pair, Share**, does every student have a well-matched partner, a clear talk goal and a set timeframe? If these details are in place, they are likely ready to move on.

3

WHERE | CONTEXT & AWARENESS

The teacher should be able to apply the technique across different contexts. Proficiency involves flexibility — can they describe how they've used the technique in other situations?

For example, if the teacher is using **Show-Me Boards**, can they explain how they've adapted the routine for both literacy and maths? If they've been working on **Live Modelling**, can they describe how it differs between their Y11 and Y7 classes?

How aware are they of the need to modify and adapt the technique? If they're not quite sure, stick at it.

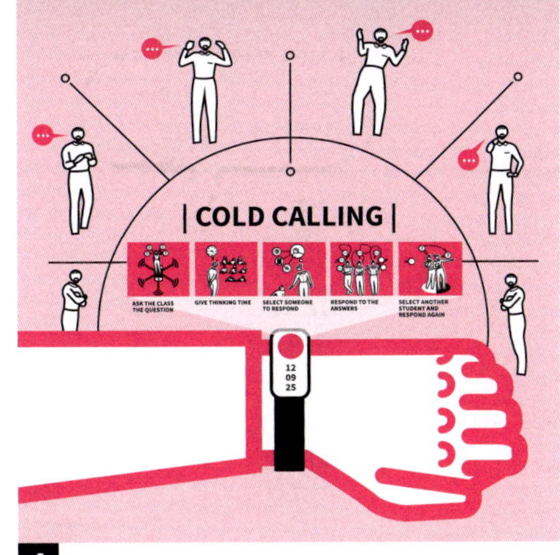

4

WHEN | TIMING & DECISION-MAKING

This is key — are they using the technique at the right moment and for the right purpose? Do they understand the decisions driving their actions and recognise when not to use the technique, avoiding unnecessary complexity or unproductive learning time?

For example, if the teacher is using **Cold Calling**, are they prompting deep thinking on core concepts rather than trivial content? Or do they make effective in-the-moment decisions to use a **Worked Example** to address misconceptions from a check for understanding?

5

HOW | TRIANGULATE & DECIDE

Triangulate the information from the previous steps. Does the teacher have a clear understanding of the why, what, where and when of using the technique, and the impact it's having in their classroom?

If any area is unclear, more work is needed. If all areas are secure, the teacher is ready to move on.

SCENARIOS

Schools and colleges face a range of real-life challenges that require coaches and leaders to be flexible, responsive and pragmatic. The Scenarios section offers practical guidance for navigating common situations — whether working with new teachers, experienced staff, large teams or colleagues who feel stuck or resistant. Each WalkThru is designed to help coaches adapt the ideas in this book to the context they're working in, while staying focused on purposeful, respectful and professional improvement.

NEW TEACHERS

Teachers at the start of their career will arrive from a variety of training settings with a range of experience, knowledge and personal confidence. It's important to acknowledge the enormous learning curve that teaching represents in the first few years while always building on what they already know and can do.

It's likely that closer support and more frequent coaching will be necessary compared to teachers with more experience.

NEW TEACHERS 162 | EXPERIENCED TEACHERS 164 | STRUGGLING TEACHERS 166 | RESISTANT TEACHER 168 | STUCK TEACHER | INGRAINED HABITS 170 | LARGE TEAMS 172 | COACHING OUTSIDE SPECIALISM 174 | COACHING PAIRS 176 |

1

SUPPORT CURRICULUM THINKING & RESOURCING

A central early challenge is to learn how the curriculum works:

- What is to be taught and in what sequence.
- How to teach key concepts and skills.
- Which resources to use.
- How assessment works.
- The appropriate pace through a learning sequence.

Subject leaders should provide the key guidance but coaches can check the teacher's confidence in accessing what they need and applying it in their lessons.

ASSERTIVENESS

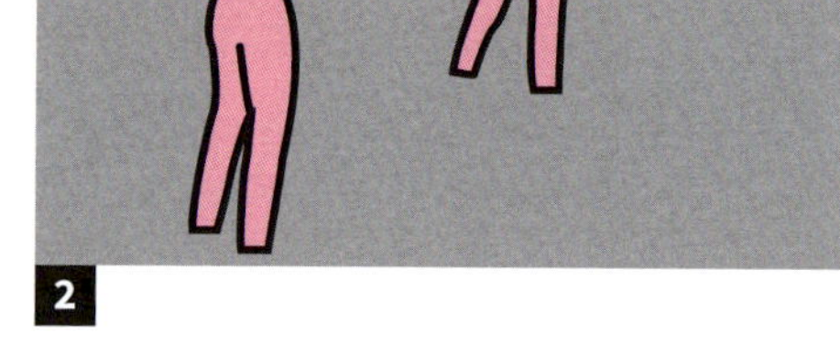

2

COACH ON CORE BEHAVIOUR TECHNIQUES

Running the room is often the most difficult part of teaching at first. Coaching should focus on:

- **Establish Your Expectations.**
- **Positive Relationships.**
- **Rehearse Routines.**
- **Assertiveness.**
- **Choices & Consequences.**

Identify specific steps, always adapting them to particular classes where challenges arise.

3

ESTABLISH GOOD HABITS WITH QUESTIONING

It's very helpful for teachers to establish good habits using core techniques they will use on most days. We'd recommend an early focus on:

- **Cold Calling.**
- **Think, Pair, Share.**
- **Show-Me Boards.**

The instinct to ask all students all the questions and not accept hands up is often not strong; the habit needs to form through intentional practice.

4

DEVELOP ROUTINES ALONGSIDE SITUATION ASSESSMENT

A tendency in coaching new teachers is to be more directive because they have a lot to learn.

However, a key part of the learning is to assess how lessons are going and make good adaptive decisions. So while helping teachers rehearse good clear routines on core techniques, always ask what they notice and what they might do differently, before sharing your expert view. Engage with their thinking and capacity to notice.

5

USE HIGH FREQUENCY CYCLES FOCUSED ON SMALL STEPS

It's vital to break down new learning into small steps, especially when there's a risk of cognitive overload.

A teacher may have multiple areas to address but a coach's skill is to help select very specific steps to focus on to have maximum impact. Higher frequency observation and coaching sessions help to keep close to the progress they make, moving them forward rapidly, building confidence.

EXPERIENCED TEACHERS

When teachers have taught for a number of years, they will have developed expertise to different degrees alongside their own teacher identity and numerous habits. They may be highly successful and self-directing.

However, as in the **Tennis Player Analogy**, they will still have capacity to improve their practice and can enjoy the coaching process. We can never assume experience leads to expertise in a simple way; teachers may have formed weak habits to unpick.

EXPER

EXPERTISE

Student outcomes

Situation awareness

Share insights

Lead coaching

Depth & detail

EXPERIENCE

1

EVALUATE EXPERTISE vs EXPERIENCE

This evaluation will be informed by observations, knowledge of student outcomes and the extent to which the teacher models good situation judgement and shares insights in a coaching session.

The more expert a teacher is, the more they will lead the coaching and the more you can explore depth and detail in techniques and how they combine. Celebrate their expertise and use **Precise Praise** to highlight where and why it lands successfully.

2

ESTABLISH GOALS & MOTIVATION

Motivation to engage with coaching depends on teachers seeing the value in it, solving problems they actually experience. An effective experienced teacher is less likely to express their goals in terms of developing their own skills: it will be more a case of improving student outcomes.

There are always some students performing less well than others and that provides a focus for the coaching.

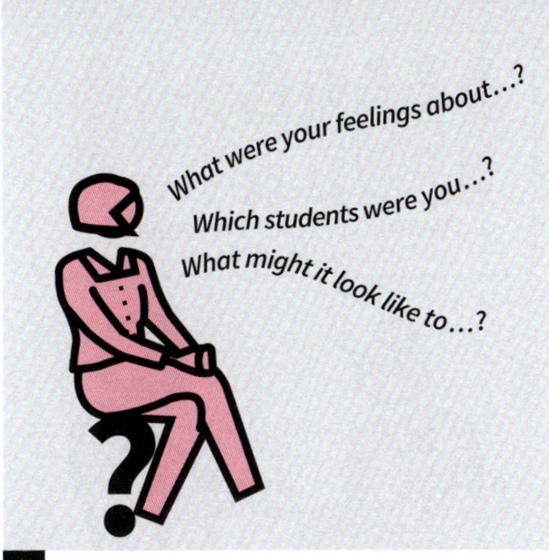

3

COACH THROUGH QUESTIONS

The *ask-don't-tell* approach is always important, but especially with an experienced teacher. The Probe element of the 5Ps invites them to share their own sense of challenges they experience. Teasing out their insights around problems and solutions can be done via questions:

- What was your feeling about the quality of outcomes from that learning sequence?
- Which students were you concerned about?
- What might it look like to get even better outcomes?

4

UNPICK FIXED HABITS

Of course many experienced teachers will have some less effective habits — e.g. accepting hands up allowing some students to dominate their lesson or insufficient checks for understanding.

Here questioning can explore details, using the WalkThrus steps as a guide.

- Looking at the WalkThru, which steps do you feel you might need to revisit?
- What impact might that have?

5

EXPLORE PRECISION & DEPTH

Often experienced, expert teachers enjoy honing their craft. It's powerful to explore details as action steps:

- The specific format of a question set for **Think, Pair, Share**, perhaps embedding **Scaffolds for Dialogue** or **Process Questions.**
- Deconstructing the elements of **Class Discussion** to ensure full engagement.
- Designing more subtle forms of **Scaffolding** to maximise success rate.

STRUGGLING TEACHERS

Any teacher might find that they struggle from time to time, so this is not a label you should ever attach to a teacher as if it is fixed.

A teacher might feel they are struggling, or leaders of teams might identify that one of their colleagues is finding it difficult to manage the flow of learning successfully across a particular class. This could be because of specific learning challenges students experience or fundamental issues with techniques.

1

IDENTIFY SPECIFIC PROBLEMS & TEACHER AWARENESS

Through observation and discussion try to pinpoint specific issues and actions that define a problem.

Turn a general sense of struggle into concrete problems to solve. For example, if a teacher says they are *having a nightmare* with a certain class:

- Why? What's happening? What might need to change? What could they say or do differently?
- Explore this with the teacher — are they noticing what you notice or do you need to point it out to them?

2

EMPATHISE, MAXIMISING EMOTIONAL SUPPORT

Try to describe the problems as inherent challenges that all teachers face — or would face if teaching that exact class. Avoid any suggestion of fault or blame.

- It's stressful if students don't seem to want to listen — what do you think we might need to do to address that?
- Yes, the curriculum really is full — what do you think we should prioritise and consolidate?

3

IDENTIFY WALKTHRUs SOLUTIONS; REVISIT TRAINING

Use WalkThrus that are familiar or very specific to the problem as a basis for coaching so that known steps can be identified and focused on. Revisit any relevant training to highlight how and why those steps work in practice.
For example, in **Signal, Pause, Insist**:

- Do you think you are communicating insistence strongly enough with that pause-insist phase?

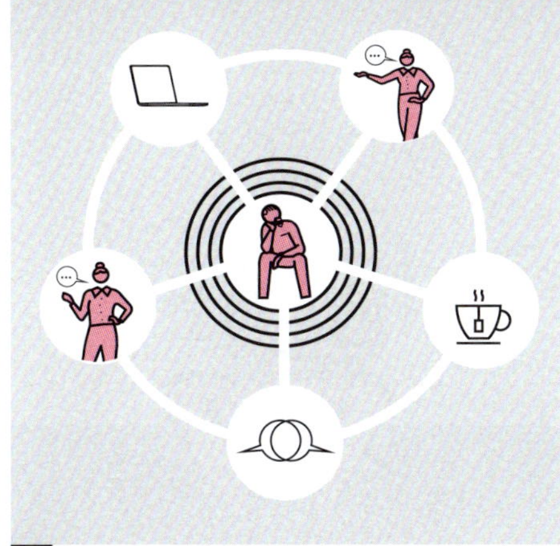

4

INCREASE COACHING FREQUENCY

A teacher who is struggling may feel isolated. They may also just want to be left alone! However, try to establish a temporary increase in coaching frequency so that you can support them to truly solve the problem — especially if they are stressed and emotional about the situation.

Multiple short visits, use of video and short coaching conversations can keep close to the detail so learning gets back on track.

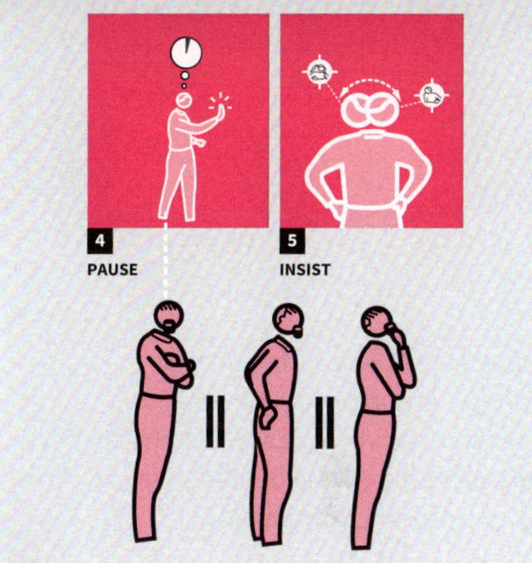

5

FOCUS ON SMALL POSITIVE GAINS

Often when a teacher is struggling, coaching needs to focus on celebrating incremental improvement, rather than a sense of fixing something broken. Improvement can be seen in:

- Introducing a step that was previously absent — e.g. the pause.
- Using the step in a more sustained way for longer or applying it to more students.
- Making an attempt to use each step in a WalkThru. If it appears mechanical at first, it's a step on the path to fluency.

RESISTANT TEACHER

This scenario is raised regularly among a group of coaches: the teacher who presents as resistant to the process, erecting obstacles or simply refusing to engage.

If we're going to engage that teacher, supporting them to develop their practice for the benefit of their student, we need to understand their perspective. Resistance is likely to be entirely understandable based on their past experiences. Cynicism or skepticism are natural dispostions to explore, not problems to eradicate. It's essential to build trust as we find a way forward.

1

ACKNOWLEDGE THEIR PERSPECTIVE

Address the resistance directly:

- I sense that you're skeptical about this process, which is understandable. Why is that exactly?
- It's not uncommon for teachers to be dubious about this at first… what's been your experience?

A candid exchange opens up dialogue and builds trust. Listen to and show respect for their position — even if you disagree with it.

2

AGREE A TRIAL PROCESS; BUY-IN WILL FOLLOW

To move forward, agree to a trial process:

- I understand your doubts but let's give this a go.

Aim to demonstrate that coaching is a constructive, affirming process, not wasting time or telling them what to do. Over time the teacher's resistance will fade in light of their postive experience.

Use the **Tennis Player Analogy**: expert players continually engage with coaching. Professional dialogue about our core practice, informed by feedback, is part of professional life where there are problems to solve.

3

FOCUS FULLY ON TEACHER'S GOALS & AREAS OF INTEREST

At first, let the teacher lead the process: they set the agenda based on their sense of themselves, the problems they have and their interests. If they won't engage when making all the choices, it's unlikely any direction will penetrate their armour.

Probe to explore their experiences, from their perspective:

- What's your area of interest in developing your practice?
- Where do you feel less than fully satisfied with how well students progress?
- What might be an interesting area to focus on?

4

FOCUS ON SELF EVALUATION & SELF-DIRECTED ACTIONS

Use **Precise Praise** liberally to provide motivational affirmation but be aware that a resistant teacher is more likely to resent being given direction and to perceive probing questions as a personal critique.

Put the ball in their court all the time:

- What was your sense of students' progress; the flow of questions?
- What might you do differently next time?
- Which students are you thinking need more support given their outcomes?
- Does this WalkThru match your sense of the technique you're using?

5

HARNESS COLLECTIVE ACTION WITHIN TEAMS

Use the power of collective action to include a resistant teacher in a process that is overtly positive. This could be in pairs, a group or a team — the other teachers often model enthusiastic engagement, which generates a sense of solidarity: we're all in it together. We're all doing this.

Engage the resistant teacher in the probing discussion, sharing their ideas about problems and solutions. Let them express dissent or concerns without judgement but then invite them to offer solutions.

STUCK TEACHER | INGRAINED HABITS

All teachers have habits that form as they repeat their many routines over time, making the process of teaching much easier. This can be incredibly helpful if the habits lead to good learning outcomes but it's problematic if the habits limit learning in some way.

Often, even if the teacher understands the need to change a habit and is motivated to do so, it is still very difficult because their existing habits are so deeply ingrained. Coaching can really help a teacher to become *unstuck*.

1

DISCUSS HABIT CHANGE EXPLICITLY

Demystify the process by discussing habit change explicitly. Peps Mccrea explores this in *Learning WalkThrus*. The trick is to break down the difference between an undesirable habit and a better habit into a set of very specific actions, then to work on enacting them deliberately and repeatedly until the new pattern of behaviour is automatic.

Reminding ourselves of the reason for the change and the benefits that will follow can help us to persist.

2

IDENTIFY THE PROBLEM HABITS

As part of the **Diagnose & Design** phase, work with the teacher to highlight where they have habits they want to change. It could be:

- Initiating questioning with 'who would like to tell me...', which invites volunteers rather than involving the whole class.
- Offering weak checks for understanding such as 'does everyone understand?'
- Not pausing to insist after giving a signal for attention.

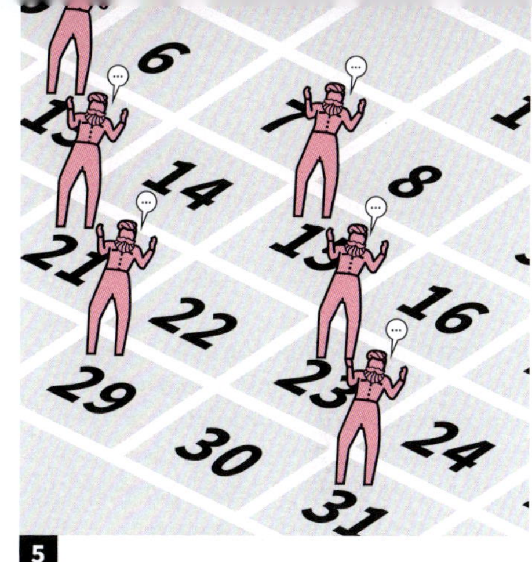

IDENTIFY BARRIERS TO CHANGE

Try to pinpoint exactly what is holding them back in breaking these habits. It could be a combination of factors:

- A feeling of awkwardness doing something they don't normally do or say.
- A lack of commitment due to a belief that it doesn't matter enough.
- Poor self-awareness in general.
- Weak knowledge of the steps in the target technique or WalkThru.

IDENTIFY & REHEARSE THE 'FIRST DOMINO'

Isolate a key change that will allow the new technique to flow. Rehearse this during the coaching with some repetition. For example:

A KEY PHRASE | *OK everyone, let's all have a think* (to unlock **Cold Calling**).

A KEY ACTION | Stand centre, still with arm raised and pause until everyone is quiet (to unlock **Signal, Pause, Insist**).

A PROMPT | Write the steps of **Think, Pair, Share** on a slide alongside the question (to ensure the *Think* part is included).

MAP OUT A VERY SHORT-TERM ACTION PLAN

A challenge with habit change is that it needs intensive effort to break the old habit and form the new one. If coaching lacks intensity, this can drag out and drift.

Make it a short change process — a sprint. Highlight specific lessons in the next days or week when the new habit will begin. Encourage daily commitment and reflection. Revisit within a short period to see progress and help sustain the motivation.

LARGE TEAMS

In **Team Conversations** we outline how the 5Ps process can be readily applied to scenarios with multiple teachers being coached simultaneously. However, the bigger the team, the more thought needs to be given to how to involve everyone.

There is a huge power in the collective action that teams generate, but there are some trade-offs that need attention and some structures that need to be present for large teams to function as a coaching unit.

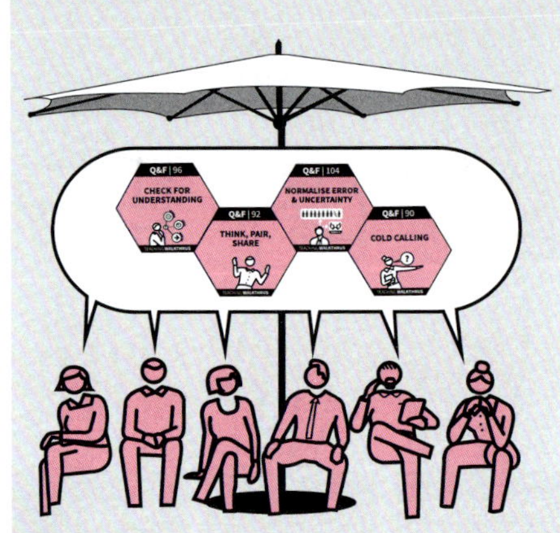

AGREE A COMMON UMBRELLA AGENDA

Although there is mileage in a small team of teachers agreeing to focus on the same thing, this is harder to sustain with a larger group. However, it is difficult if everyone is doing their own thing — that's too fragmented for a meaningful discussion.

Agree a broader umbrella of issues that allow degrees of freedom — e.g. **Checks for Understanding**, which includes **Show-Me Boards, Show Calling** and **Guided Practice.**

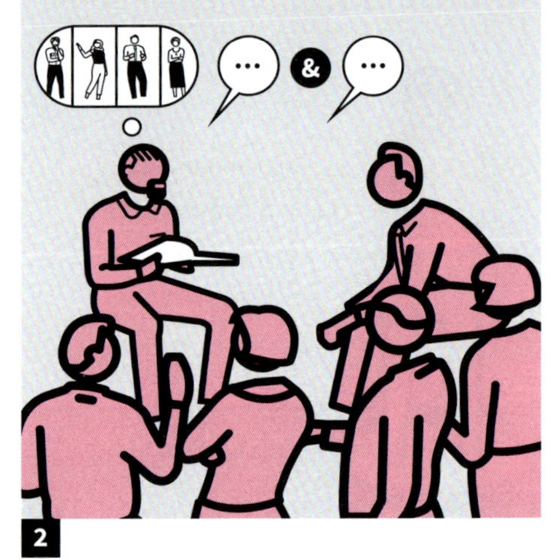

2

SAMPLE LESSONS EACH CYCLE

With a large team, it's more difficult to be sure the leader can complete learning walks or drop-ins for every individual teacher themselves. The key is to sample the practice in order to provide reality-check feedback in each session:

- Share the observations among leaders and others.
- Invite teachers to use video or peer observation as well.
- Just sample as many lesson as possible without visting everyone each cycle.

SYSTEMATICALLY INVOLVE EVERYONE WITH PAIR TALK

During the Precise Praise and Probe phases of **Team Conversations**, everyone must be involved.

The best approach is to divide people into pairs and engage them in discussion where each person shares their ideas. Invite pairs to then share key elements of their discussion with the whole team. They don't all have to share at this point — the key thing is that they have done the thinking and exchanged this with someone. The **Class Discussion** WalkThru works superbly well here.

4

AGREE INDIVIDUAL TARGETS WITHIN SUB-TEAMS

Having aired the issues and explored some specific problems to focus on, it can be tedious to go around the table so each member of a team can state their personal action step.

This part is better done by breaking the team into pairs or threes within which each teacher states their planned action steps and perhaps records them on their personal log. The team leader may or may not need to collate each person's steps but that's easy to do with shared documents.

5

ADDRESS PRESSING INDIVIDUAL ISSUES SEPARATELY

Of course, in a large team, there will be some individuals who will struggle at times in a personal way such that it would be inappropriate and ineffective to support them within a team context.

Here, periods of one-to-one coaching and support might be needed, dovetailing with the team process. They can still benefit from the solidarity and motivational drive that teams provide while having more personal matters addressed separately on their own.

COACHING OUTSIDE SPECIALISM

A very common scenario in coaching is that the coach is not a specialist in the subject of the teacher they are coaching. Sometimes this is by design: a coach is allocated a caseload of coachees from across the staff body. Sometimes it is from necessity — there isn't enough capacity for subject-specific coaching by a specialist. Sometimes a senior leader acts as the coach and has a different subject background.

This can work extremely well provided that the coach adopts the disposition of the non-expert asking questions, looking and learning, not judging and directing. We've had success ourselves coaching across every conceivable subject.

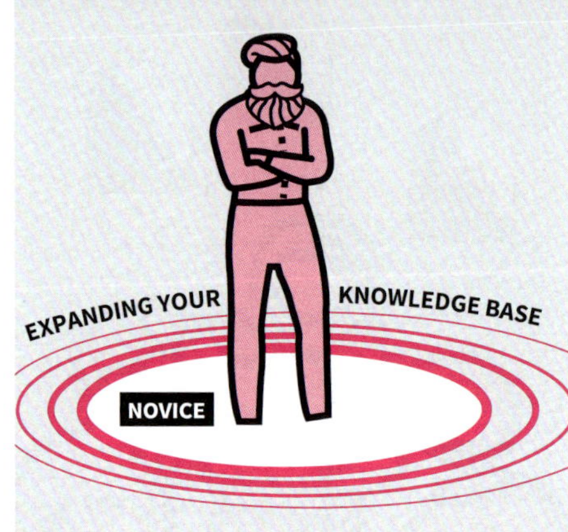

1

ACCEPT YOUR LIMITS; DEVELOP KNOWLEDGE OVER TIME

Acknowledge the limits of your expertise within the coaching process. Never make directive suggestions that have a curriculum origin in a different subject — it could be a terrible idea.

Begin by assuming the position of a total novice, only asking questions and seeking clarification in relation to curriculum specifics.

Over time, try to build up your knowledge of the discipline. Study the curriculum and assessment regimes and, where possible, observe multiple lessons in that area.

2

PROBE | INTENTIONS AND STANDARDS

Good probing questions might include:

- Did the lesson flow as you intended? Is that a typical kind of lesson for you?
- What would excellence have looked like in that lesson?
- Where were you thinking it wasn't going quite as well as you'd have liked in terms of students' outcomes?
- What would it look like to push the challenge level higher? Are any of the students ready for that?
- What might you change when you do that lesson again?

3

PROBE | STUDENT PROGRESS AND RESPONSE

You can always focus on individuals:

- *Were there any students you were particularly pleased by/ concerned about?*
- *I noticed James gave a long answer — was that the type of response you were looking for?*
- *I noticed that Sam was struggling a bit — from what he told me. Is that a pattern? What kind of help might he need?*
- *The girl near me was only half way through the exercise when you stopped the class — is that what you'd expect? Does that have implications for the task design for her?*

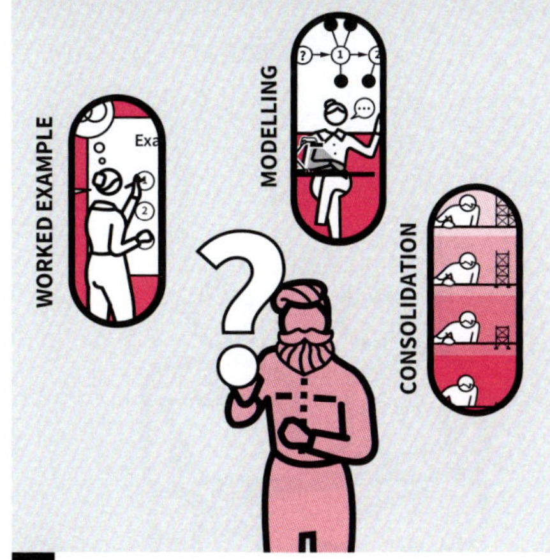

4

TRUST YOUR JUDGEMENT BUT ONLY OFFER SUGGESTIONS

With due humility for your lack of specialist subject knowledge, you can still offer suggestions based on your general understanding of learning.

- *Do you mind if I ask — would it help to go through more fully worked examples before asking students to practise?*
- *I was wondering if maybe the length of the modelled writing was too long for some students to then emulate on their own — but what's your sense of that?*
- *If felt to me like they needed a bit more time to practise and consolidate — but I don't know what's typical. What did you think?*

5

LINK INTO TEAM PROCESSES

Coach fully aware that the teacher is in a team that sets the curriculum agenda. As a non-expert, tap into that and build the coaching process to support or complement it. If general behaviour or pedagogical issues arise you can address them with confidence.

Find out what the team agenda is and ask questions around it.

- *What's your priority in this lesson sequence, curriculum-wise?*
- *What are the main issues you're trying to address as a team?*
- *How well do you think you're doing in enacting the team agenda at the moment?*

COACHING PAIRS

Coaching in pairs is one of the possibilities covered in **Coaching Configurations.** Here we explore this particular scenario further because it is a popular option that works extremely well, especially when the teachers work in the same year group or primary phase or teach in the same subject team. This allows conversations to link to curriculum and for the dialogue to extend beyond the coaching sessions.

As well as halving the number of meetings needed, the dynamics of the sessions can lead to a deeper exploration of the issues, and the collective element helps fuel motivation and commitment to habit change.

1

PLAN CYCLES IN ADVANCE

With calendar to hand, map out the school year in terms of coaching cycles taking account of teachers' availability in the timetable. With pairs it can be relatively easy to find time in the school week to form a regular coaching slot where coach and both teachers can meet. If not, choose an after-school meeting time to serve as the coaching slot. Aim for a frequency of 2-4 weeks across the year.

The coach might be a senior leader, team leader or specialist coach.

2

MIX MODES OF OBSERVATION

Plan time for observation at each session so that subsequent sessions are informed by a reality check for both teachers. With pairs it is possible — and perhaps more interesting — to use a variety of observation modes over a term or year:

- The coach observes each teacher — probably the dominant mode.
- The pair of teachers observe each other, with lesson cover if needed.
- Each teacher records a video of themselves doing their action step.
- Paired observation: coach plus teacher co-observe the other teacher.

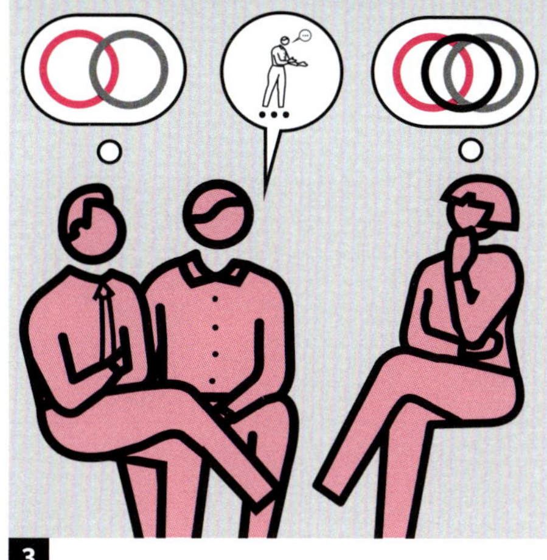

3

DIAGNOSE COMMON ISSUES TO EXPLORE

Use the first session to diagnose issues arising from the observations, looking for common ground. This could be related to a specific unit of work, a teaching technique or a common problem such as engaging all students in responses to modelling or **Cold Calling**. Let the teachers lead this discussion, supporting them to share ideas openly.

(It's very rare for there to be no common ground or a radically different urgent agenda for each teacher — but if there is, you may need to do some individual coaching alongside.)

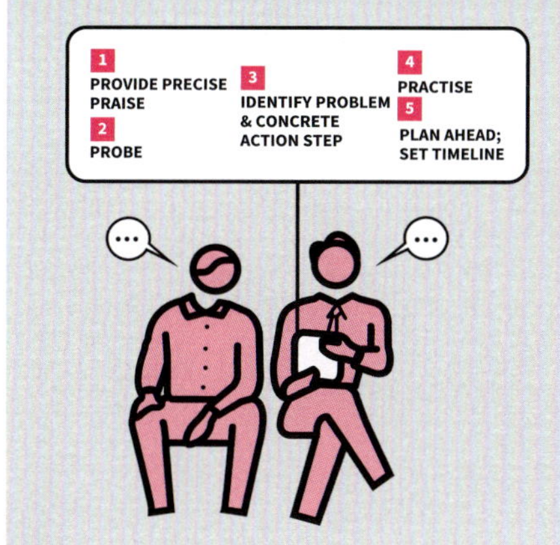

4

RUN THE 5Ps FEEDBACK TOGETHER

The key to paired coaching being effective is that there is a discipline in following the feedback process with real integrity when more than one person is involved. Each teacher serves as an audience to the other; the coach is aware that each interaction is modelling behaviours and language to both teachers to use with each other.

- Use Precise Praise to establish common strengths and areas of confidence.
- Probe to establish where things are challenging or need to be practised further.
- Explore a full range of common problems.

5

AGREE ACTION STEPS INDIVIDUALLY WITHIN THE PAIR

At the end of the coaching session, ensure both teachers have committed to an action step they will focus on in the subsequent cycle.

It could be the same step for both — if they feel that helps them — or it could be a different one. In the pair, ask each teacher in turn to run through their plan of action with specifics about the class, students or curriculum material.

Record the action steps on a shared document and then run the cycle again, following the agreed plan and mode of reality check.

Bambrick-Santoyo, P.	2018	Leverage Leadership 2.0: A Practical Guide to Building Exceptional Schools	Jossey-Bass, San Fransisco, US	book
Banks, B., Sims, S., Curran, J., Meliss, S., Chowdhury, N., Altunbas, H. G., Alexandri, N., MacTavish, L. & Instone, I.	2024	Decomposition and Recomposition: Effects on Novice Teachers' Enactment and Transfer of Behaviour Management Practices.	https://www.ambition.org.uk/research-decomposition-and-recomposition/	online
Breakspear, S. & Jones, B. R.	2019	Teaching Sprints: How Overloaded Educators Can Keep Getting Better	Corwin, Thousand Oaks, California, US	book
Bungay Stanier, M.	2016	The Coaching Habit: Say Less, Ask More & Change the Way You Lead Forever	Box of Crayons Press, Toronto, Ontario, Canada	book
Clear, J.	2018	Atomic Habits	Penguin Random House, US	book
Costa, A. & Garmston, R.	2016	Cognitive Coaching: Developing Self-Directed Leaders and Learners (3rd ed.)	Rowman & Littlefield Publishers, US	book
Danielson, C.	2009	Talk About Teaching!: Leading Professional Conversations	Corwin, Thousand Oaks, California, US	book
Duarte, N.	2012	HBR Guide to Persuasive Presentations	Harvard Business Review Press, US	book
Education Endowment Foundation	2021	Effective Professional Development	https://educationendowmentfoundation.org.uk/education-evidence/guidance-reports/effective-professional-development	online
Gawande, A.	2009	The Checklist Manifesto: How to Get Things Right	Henry Holt & Co., New York, US	book
Goodrich, J.	2024	Responsive Coaching	Hodder Education, UK	book
Goodwin, C.	1994	Professional Vision	American Anthropologist; https://www.researchgate.net/publication/227980682_Professional_Vision	online
Grinder, M.	2012	Charisma: The Art of Relationships	Michael Grinder & Associates	book
Grossman, P. et al.	2009	Teaching Practice: A Cross-Professional Perspective	https://www.researchgate.net/publication/265357624_Teaching_Practice_A_Cross-Professional_Perspective	online
Heath, C. & Heath, D.	2007	Made to Stick: Why Some Ideas Survive and Others Die	Random House, US	book

Kennedy, M.	1999	The Role of Preservice Teacher Education	https://www.scribd.com/document/211371753/Mary-Kennedy-1999-Role-of-Preservice-Teacher-Education-Problem-of-Enactment	online
Kennedy, M.	2016a	How Does Professional Development Improve Teaching?	https://www.researchgate.net/publication/292675761_How_Does_Professional_Development_Improve_Teaching	online
Kennedy, M.	2016b	Parsing the Practice of Teaching	https://www.researchgate.net/publication/283800050_Parsing_the_Practice_of_Teaching	online
Knight, J.	2018	The Impact Cycle	Corwin, Thousand Oaks, California, US	book
Knight, J.	2021	The Definitive Guide to Instructional Coaching: Seven Factors for Success	ASCD, Alexandria, US	
Lemov, D.	2021	Teach Like a Champion 3.0	Jossey-Bass, San Fransisco, US	book
Lunzer, E. & Gardner, K.	1984	Learning from the Written Word	Oliver & Boyd, Edinburgh, UK	book
Pontis, S. & Babwahsingh, M.	2024	Information Design Unbound	Bloomsbury, London, UK	book
Robinson, V.	2017	Reduce Change to Increase Improvement	Corwin, Thousand Oaks, California, US	book
Rosenshine, B.	2012	Principles of Instruction	https://unesdoc.unesco.org/ark:/48223/pf0000190652	online
Schank, R. C. & Abelson, R.P.	1977	Scripts, Plans, Goals & Understanding	http://www.colinallen.dnsalias.org/Readings/1977-SchankAbelson.pdf	online
Sherrington, T. & Caviglioli, O.	2020	Teaching WalkThrus	Hachette Learning, UK	book
Sherrington, T. & Caviglioli, O.	2021	Teaching WalkThrus 2	Hachette Learning, UK	book
Sherrington, T. & Caviglioli, O.	2022	Teaching WalkThrus 3	Hachette Learning, UK	book
Stone, D. & Heen, S.	2014	Thanks for the Feedback: The Science and Art of Receiving Feedback Well	Viking, New York, US	book
Sweller, J., Ayres, P. & Kalyuga, S.	2011	Cognitive Load Theory	Springer, New York, US	book
Wiliam, D.	2012	Embedding Formative Assessment	Solution Tree Press, Bloomington, US	book
Willingham, D. T.	2009	Why Don't Students Like School?	Jossey-Bass, San Fransisco, US	book
Wood, W.	2019	Good Habits, Bad Habits: The Science of Making Positive Changes That Stick	Pan Macmillan, UK	book

JOIN OUR WALKTHRU COMMUNITY

If you want to integrate coaching into the fabric of our organisation, then WalkThrus membership provides all the tools and resources you need. You'll be joining a dynamic community of thousands of member schools in 50+ countries. Use the QR code to find out more. We look forward to welcoming you.

Take me to the WalkThrus website and membership information.

HOW WOULD YOU BUILD A SHARED UNDERSTANDING OF TEACHING?

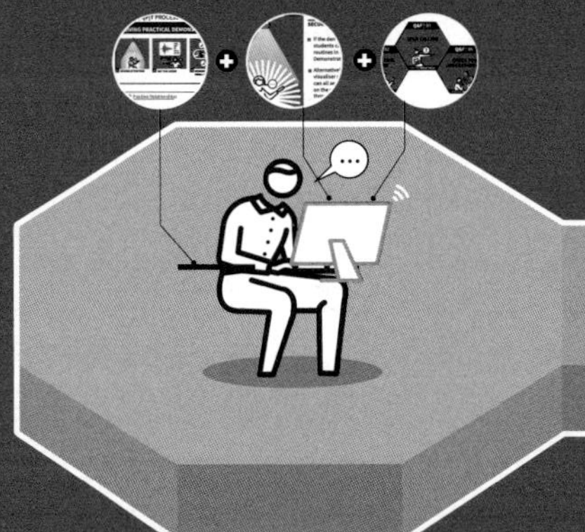

TEACHING WALKTHRUS RESOURCES

The WalkThrus playbooks are the most comprehensive capture of the best teaching techniques. Their methodical organisation, clear descriptions and illustrations offer your coaches a tested route to gain this essential knowledge.

HOW WOULD YOU TRAIN UP YOUR COACHES?

ACCREDITED COURSES

The WalkThrus suite of courses cover coaching, training, consultancy and system leadership. Integrating different levels of system activity leads to a more aligned and successful approach that sustains momentum over the years.

HOW WOULD YOU IMPLEMENT COACHING CYCLES?

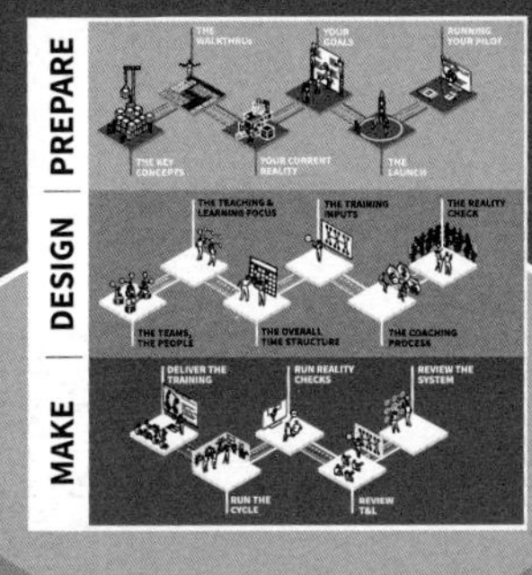

P|D|M IMPLEMENTATION GUIDES

Developed from years of fieldwork in schools and colleges, the Prepare It, Design It and Make It Happen models help you create your own bespoke trajectory based on what we've found really works in practice. Consistently so.

HOW WOULD YOU IMPLEMENT COACHING CYCLES?

COACHING WALKTHRUS RESOURCES

Slide decks of all the WalkThrus in this book, supported by Trainer Notes, ensure your presentations will be effective. The confidence and authority you gain from these resources should not be underestimated.

HOW WOULD YOU DELIVER EXCELLENT TRAINING?

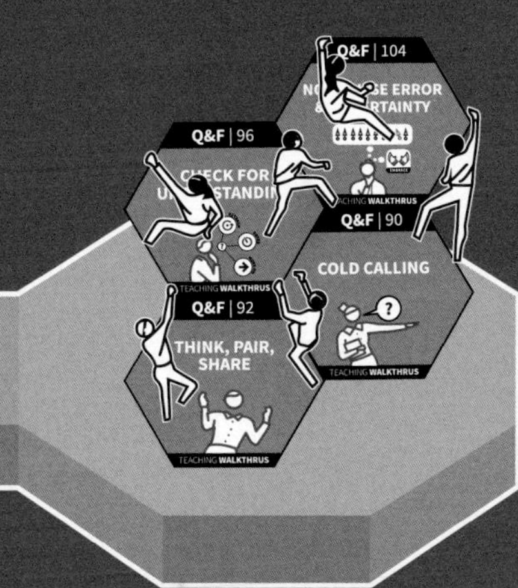

CLUSTER BUILDER

Effective performance consists of fluent sequences of actions. In teaching, we have clusters designed into coaching conversations and customised to an infinite range of configurations. This is a unique feature of the WalkThrus.